HISTORY
OF THE
ARMENIANS IN INDIA

HISTORY
OF THE
ARMENIANS IN INDIA

From the Earliest Times to the Present Day.

BY

MESROVB J. SETH,

ARMENIAN EXAMINER TO THE UNIVERSITY OF CALCUTTA.

GYAN

Published by

GYAN

Gyan Publishing House
5, Ansari Road
Daryaganj, New Delhi-110002
Phone: 011-47034999, 9811692060
E-mail: books@gyanbooks.com

Distribution Network
gyanbooks.com
India, USA, Canada, UK, Australia, France

ISBN: 978-81-212-0187-2 (HB)

Reprint in India, 2024
First Published, 2018

Printed at: Gyan Press, Delhi.

History of the Armenians in India:
From the Earliest Times to the Present Day
Author: Mesrovb J. Seth

PREFACE.

THE history of the Armenian nation, since the loss of its political independence in the fourteenth century, after the death at Paris in 1393 of Leo VI., the last Armenian king, is one of the darkest epochs in its national history and has perhaps no parallel in the annals of any nation. It presents one long series of barbarities and atrocities perpetrated on them by their inveterate foes—the Saracens, the Tartars, the Persians and the 'unspeakable Turk,'—who have in turn led their bloodthirsty hordes into Armenia, indiscriminately murdered its inhabitants, pillaged and devastated their flourishing cities, and (in the words of Byron) "desolated the region where God created man in His own image."

These invasions naturally served to scatter the Armenian nation; and, leaving their homes in large numbers, they migrated to other countries where, in the enjoyment of security of life and property, they soon formed important colonies and distinguished themselves in their commercial pursuits. The interesting history of the various Armenian colonies in European and Asiatic countries, forms one of the brightest in the otherwise dark pages of the history of the Armenian nation for the past five hundred years. A lover of history, I have always taken a keen interest in the history of these once-flourishing colonies, about which there is, however, but very little on record. My favourite hobby has been the history of the various Armenian colonies in India and the Far East, fostered no doubt by the various narratives I have heard from my venerable father (now in his seventy-fifth year), to whom I am greatly indebted for having instilled into my youthful heart a taste for antiquarian knowledge and research and an ardent love for the rich classical Armenian literature.

Being anxious to gather further information regarding the Armenian colonists in India, I ransacked our modest ancestral library, which was rich in Armenian publications, printed at Madras, where my grandfather had been a merchant for several years in the second half of the eighteenth century. I next turned my attention to the numerous Armenian letters in my father's *escretoire*, which were written to my great-grandfather (Mackertich Agazar Seth) at Julfa by my grandfather and other Armenian merchants, chiefly from Surat and Madras, during the last century, and some contained materials of historical value. These, with a number of other important documents and MSS., I brought from Julfa as valuable relics, intending some day to utilize them in a historical work. On arriving at Calcutta in

1889, to complete my education, I endeavoured while at school to gather information regarding the early Armenians in this country. At the outset I was disappointed, there being no archives or any library in Calcutta containing books and MSS. in the Armenian language, and the Araratean Library at the Armenian College and Philanthropic Academy, where I studied, had on its shelves but a few unimportant printed volumes (see page 178, footnote). "There is nothing on record about them!" was the general response to my enquiries from everyone.

Next I consulted every available English historian of India from Orme to Marshman and Hunter, but found only a few references to individual Armenians. Extracts from these and other writers on India have been given in this work. The interesting *Ain-i-Akbari*, compiled in 1596 by Abul Fazl, the learned finance minister of Akbar the Great, and other Muhammadan histories of India were searched with no better results. After great difficulty, I procured complete sets of some of the Armenian journals published from time to time in India, and from these I was able to glean considerable fragmentary information, and afterwards a few manuscripts and letters in Armenian, connected with India, came into my possession.

Another field remained practically unexplored, namely, the interesting inscriptions in the Armenian burying-grounds. I had, it is true, obtained copies of a few important Armenian inscriptions from some of the places where Armenians had lived and died, and had been over the Armenian burying-grounds at Calcutta and Chinsurah; but I had a longing to see with my own eyes the tombs of the departed at Agra, Gwalior, Surat, Bombay, Masulipatam, Madras, Dacca, Syedabad, Patna, and other centres of Armenian commerce. Some of these places I have since visited, and have had the pleasure of studying, *in situ*, these valuable landmarks of Armenians.

My object in collecting antiquarian information regarding the Armenians was to place on record, at some future period, the result of my researches, as a small contribution to Armenian history. My idea originally was to publish my notes in the Armenian language, but I was induced to produce them in English under the following auspicious circumstances.

Early in 1894 the local Government had, at the instance of the Government of India, compiled a list of the old Christian tombs and monuments in Bengal possessing historical or archæological interest; and a few months later I was asked by the Bengal Government to translate into English a number of classical Armenian inscriptions on the tombstones in the Armenian churchyards at Calcutta, Chinsurah (a suburb of Hooghly), and Syedabad (a suburb of Murshidabad), for incorporation in that list. While engaged in that interesting work, which helped to stimulate my antiquarian proclivities, I decided upon preparing a brief historical sketch in English of the various Armenian colonies in India. In January 1895 I left for Hyderabad (Deccan), visiting Bombay *en route*. During my short stay I copied all the inscriptions in the Armenian churchyard and the old cemetery at Bombay, and also some sequestered ones at Byculla, its suburb, in the compound of a private dwelling-house.

On returning to Calcutta shortly afterwards, I had the happiness of forming the acquaintance of Mr. C. R. Wilson, M.A., Professor of Mental and Moral Philosophy and Logic in the Presidency College, Calcutta, and Secretary of the Asiatic Society of Bengal, in connection with the valuable discovery referred to on pages 39 to 41, which had aroused his antiquarian enthusiasm. I may mention that he took the keenest interest in the excavation of the Old Fort of Calcutta in 1891, and took pains to locate the exact site of the historical Black Hole. The result of his discoveries will be found in an appendix to the latest edition of Newman & Co.'s *Handbook to Calcutta*. I am glad to embrace this opportunity of cordially thanking the erudite professor for his valuable assistance; for he was pleased to place at my disposal certain valuable extracts from the early records of the Hon'ble East India Company which are preserved in the archives of the East India House in London. These extracts, now published for the first time, are of inestimable value from a historical point of view, for they shed a flood of light on the history of the Company's all-important deputation to the Mogul Court at Delhi in 1715, in which Khojah Israel Sarhad, an Armenian merchant, played a prominent part, and by his tact and diplomacy succeeded in securing for the English the *Grand Firman* from the Emperor Ferokhsiyar.

I am also indebted to the *Calcutta Review*, from which some valuable extracts have been taken, and to the *Englishman* for its eulogistic reference to my fortunate discovery of the oldest Christian tomb in Calcutta. The other sources from which I have derived information have been duly acknowledged.

The sun seemed at last to shine upon my endeavours. I was fortunate in procuring a copy of the now comparatively rare *Considerations on India Affairs* by "William Bolts, Merchant, and Alderman or Judge of the Hon'ble The Mayor's Court of Calcutta." This valuable work, which was published at London in 1772, contained much interesting information regarding the Armenians in Bengal, and several extracts from it have been reproduced here.

The dreadful tragedy enacted by the Turkish and Kurdish soldiery at Sassoon, Armenia, in the autumn of 1894, on defenceless Armenians, aroused the sympathy and shocked the feelings of the entire Christian world. The massacres and atrocities perpetrated were of so horrible a nature, that Mr. Gladstone, Armenia's truest friend, in addressing the Anglo-Armenian deputation at Hawarden on the anniversary of his eighty-fifth birthday, 29th December 1894, gave expression to the following memorable words:—

"Now, it is certainly true that we have not arrived at the close of this inquiry, and I will say nothing to assume that the allegations will be verified. At the same time, I cannot pretend to say that there is no reason to anticipate an unfavorable issue. On the contrary, the intelligence which has reached me tends to a conclusion which I still hope may not be verified, but tends strongly to a conclusion to the general effect that the outrages and the scenes and abominations of 1876 in Bulgaria have been repeated in 1894 in Armenia. As I have said, I hope it is not so, and I will hope to the last, but if it is so, it is time that one general shout of execration, not of men, but of deeds, one general shout of execration directed against deeds of wickedness, should rise from outraged humanity, and should force itself into the ears of the Sultan of Turkey and make him sensible, if anything can make him sensible, of the madness of such a course."

Universal sympathy was felt for the helpless Armenians under Turkish misrule, for their lives, honour, and property were daily at the fiendish mercy of their oppressors, the Kurds and the Turks. Mass meetings were accordingly convened throughout Europe, eloquent speeches delivered, the usual number of resolutions passed, and the Great Powers were petitioned. Not only this, but subscriptions were opened and funds were raised for the relief of the destitute and homeless survivors. The Armenians everywhere mourned the loss of their martyred brethren at Sassoon, and special prayers were said and a *requiem* service held, for the repose of their souls, at all Armenian churches throughout the world. The Armenian community of Calcutta convened a meeting on 21st January 1895, at the Theatre Royal, to which sympathizers of other nationalities were invited, "for the purpose of taking into consideration the recent sad events in Turkish Armenia." Several resolutions were passed, and in due course a petition was drawn up and sent to England and the other signatory Powers of the Treaty of Berlin. A subscription was also opened here for the relief of distressed Armenians in Turkey, which was liberally subscribed to, not only by the Armenians, but by the leading European mercantile and trading houses.

Hopes were entertained that the Great Powers would force Turkey to carry out the much-needed reforms in Armenia; but it was to England that the Armenians chiefly looked for help and deliverance from the iron yoke of the Turk, which threatened to crush, if not annihilate, them. Not until the country was in a state of anarchy, and after a series of terrible massacres, in which defenceless Armenians were mercilessly butchered, have the Powers and America shown their practical sympathy by despatching ironclads to the Levant. Their concerted action has aroused the Sultan from his lethargy, and he has hysterically pledged his "word of honour" (!) that he will personally see the necessary reforms carried out in Armenia. But His Majesty's promises heretofore have not been followed by performances; and, as Lord Salisbury shrewdly observes, "New decrees cannot supply the place of competent Governors." The Powers are now at his door, and we may soon expect the inauguration of wholesale reforms, but it is to be hoped the peace of Europe will not be disturbed.

A strong interest having been aroused in the Armenians in Turkey, my friends prevailed upon me to publish the result of my researches regarding the early Armenians in India, as information respecting them was but scanty. The present work, prepared during the sultry nights of the enervating Indian summer, is the result. It has doubtless several shortcomings, for I have had to *think* in Armenian, and express my ideas in English. History, however, does not hinge upon philosophy, but on facts; and it is far more important to preserve accuracy than study flowery language in a historical work.

I trust this history will serve some useful purpose as a book of reference to the future historian of India and the enthusiastic antiquarian; and I shall be greatly gratified if it acts as an incentive to the present generation of Armenians in India to emulate the strong piety and patriotism that animated their ancestors. Then I shall feel rewarded; for, in the words of my mentor, the immortal Mesrovb David Thaliatin, "it is the duty of the true patriot to revive the spirit of the children by the example of the illustrious deeds of their ancestors."

MESROVB J. SETH.

WELLESLEY SQUARE, E., CALCUTTA,
November 1895.

CONTENTS.

CHAPTER I.

HISTORICAL SKETCH OF THE ARMENIAN NATION.

CHAPTER II.

ADVENT OF THE ARMENIANS INTO INDIA.

CHAPTER III.

LANDMARKS OF ARMENIANS IN BEHAR AND BENGAL.

CHAPTER IV.

ARMENIANS AND THE EAST INDIA COMPANY.

CHAPTER V.

ARMENIANS AS POLITICAL STEPPING-STONES.

CHAPTER VI.

BRITISH SUPREMACY IN THE ASCENDANT.

CHAPTER VII.

BOLTS DENOUNCES THE COMPANY'S POLICY.

CHAPTER VIII.

MONOPOLY OF SALT, BETEL-NUT AND TOBACCO.

CHAPTER IX.

TWO ARMENIANS OF WEALTH AND HONOUR.

CHAPTER X.

HOW ARMENIAN LOYALTY WAS REWARDED IN PROSPERITY AND ADVERSITY.

CHAPTER XI.

ARMENIAN LITERARY INSTITUTIONS, ETC.

CHAPTER XII.

THE ARMENIAN SETTLEMENT IN SOUTHERN INDIA.

CHAPTER XIII.

AN OLLA PODRIDA OF INTERESTING EVENTS.

CHAPTER XIV.

PROMULGATION OF ARMENIAN LITERATURE IN INDIA.

CHAPTER XV.

CONCLUSION.

APPENDICES.

APPENDIX A—THE CLASSICAL ARMENIAN LANGUAGE.

APPENDIX B—A NEGLECTED CLASSICAL LANGUAGE.

"*By nature the Armenians are deeply religious, as their whole literature and history show. It has been a religion of the heart, not of the head. Its evidence is not to be found in metaphysical discussions and hair-splitting theology, as in the case of the Greeks, but in a brave and simple record written with the tears of saints and illuminated with the blood of martyrs.*"— 'THE ARMENIAN CRISIS AND THE RULE OF THE TURK,' by the Rev. Frederick Davis Greene, M.A., for several years a resident in Armenia.

HISTORY

OF THE

ARMENIANS IN INDIA.

"*It would be difficult, perhaps, to find the annals of a nation less stained with crimes than those of the Armenians, whose virtues have been those of peace, and their vices those of compulsion.*"—BYRON.

CHAPTER I.

HISTORICAL SKETCH OF THE ARMENIAN NATION.

BEFORE proceeding with the history of the Armenians in India, I purpose, in this introductory chapter, giving the reader a brief insight into the origin and early history of the Armenians in their primitive home in the country of Ararat of Biblical renown; for more than one modern English writer has disseminated erroneous impressions regarding the Armenian nation, and, so little have some of them been in touch with their subject, that they have represented the Armenians as a *religious* sect or as a *commercial* community!

Descended from the common Aryan stock, their existence as a nation dates as far back as the year 2111 B.C., when Haik assumed the supremacy.

That the Armenians are much older than the Jews *as a nation*, is evident from the historical fact that HAIK,* the patriarch and founder of the Armenian nation, was born in the year 2277 B.C., whereas ABRAHAM† was born in the year 1996 B.C., nearly three centuries later. Haik was the fifth in descent from Noah; Abraham, the eleventh. The antiquity of the Armenian nation is attested by Herodotus, Strabo, and other ancient writers; and still further by the interesting cuneiform inscriptions on the celebrated Rock of Van in Armenia, which have been deciphered by that learned Englishman, Professor Sayce.

Several references are made in the book of Genesis to the country inhabited by the Armenians; and it is beyond doubt that the Garden of Eden was planted in Armenia, since the four rivers, *viz.*, Pison (Jorokh), Gihon (Araxes), Hiddekel (Tigris), and the Euphrates (Gen. ii. 11-14), which once watered the earthly Paradise, still flow through that region. According to Holy Writ, the Ark of Noah, after the Deluge, rested "upon the mountains of Ararat," and on the plains below "Noah builded an altar unto the Lord," whereon he "offered burnt-offerings" (Gen. viii. 20): thus showing that the *first* altar was erected in Armenia. On His reconciliation with mankind, God placed

---

* *Genealogy of Haik.*

Haik was the son of		Togarmah.
Togarmah	,,	Gomer.
Gomer	,,	Japheth.
Japheth	,,	Noah.
		(Gen. x. 2, 3.)

† *Genealogy of Abraham.*

Abraham was the son of		Terah.
Terah	,,	Nahor.
Nahor	,,	Serug.
Serug	,,	Reu.
Reu	,,	Peleg.
Peleg	,,	Eber.
Eber	,,	Salah.
Salah	,,	Arphaxad.
Arphaxad	,,	Shem.
Shem	,,	Noah.
		(Gen. xi. 10-26.)

the rainbow in the cloud "for a token of a covenant" between Him and the earth: thus the bow was seen for the *first* time in the horizon that encompassed the gorgeous country of Ararat. Noah settled with his household at the foot of the Ararat mountains, and in its virgin soil planted the vine, which grows so luxuriantly in Armenia even to this day; he drank of the wine thereof, "and was drunken": thus the vine was *first* planted and grown in Armenia.

The fertile plain of Ararat therefore became the cradle of the human race after the Deluge, where Noah settled with his sons, who multiplied and peopled the country. In course of time, with increasing population, migration followed. The people were "of one language and of one speech," and some journeyed towards Shinar in Mesopotamia. Among these was Haik, a local chief, who became the ancestor and founder of the Armenian nation. Haik, after whom Armenians call themselves 'Haiks' (*i.e.*, Armenians) and their country 'Haiastan' (*i.e.*, Armenia), was a great-grandson of Noah, the 'Just Man,' being the son of Thorgomah (Togarmah, Gen. x. 3), son of Gomer, son of Japheth, the eldest son of Noah. According to Armenian historians, Haik was brave, handsome, magnanimous, and a skilful archer of considerable strength, and probably was one of the builders of the Tower on the plain of Shinar, whose top was to reach "unto heaven" (Gen. xi. 4).

After the destruction of that masterpiece of primitive architecture on the Euphrates, and the dispersion of the nations consequent on the confusion of tongues, Haik, unwilling to submit to the authority of Belus, the Nimrod of the Bible, who ruled supreme at Babel (*i.e.*, Babylon), turned his steps towards the land of his birth with his entire household, which numbered 300 persons exclusive of servants, and a host of other followers from Mesopotamia who had attached themselves to him. On returning to his fatherland, Haik settled with his household and followers in the vicinity of Ararat. He then subjugated a number of people then living there, and was acknowledged by them as their chief and patriarch.

When Belus heard that Haik had founded a nation, and had thereby shaken off allegiance to him, he sent a deputation recalling him to submission. That, however, produced no effect upon Haik, and Belus thereupon assembled all his warriors, whose name was legion, and marched against him. On being informed of the arrival of Belus in South Armenia by his grandson Cadmus, whom he had settled in that part of the country, Haik summoned his comparatively small band of warriors, and went to meet the powerful invader from Mesopotamia. The armies met and fought, Belus was repulsed, and, in retreating, fell by a shaft from the heavy bow of Haik; the arrow, penetrating the thick brazen breastplate, passed through his body, killing him on the spot. Thus perished the Nimrod of Holy Writ, aged 200 years, who was "a mighty one in the earth," and also "a mighty hunter before the Lord" (Gen. x. 8, 9). This occurred in the year 2108 B.C. Now free, after this signal victory, from his powerful foe, Haik founded a nation and a monarchy which was destined to be a vast empire, and play an important part in the arena of the old world. He died in the year 2031 B.C., aged 246 years.

This, briefly, is the origin of the Armenian nation, which was founded in the year 2111 B.C. by Haik, the great national hero: it is not therefore mythical, or shrouded in impenetrable darkness, as is the case with many a nation of antiquity.

Even in the days of Abraham, the Armenians were a powerful nation. Alexander Polyhistor, a Greek writer and historian, affirms that the Armenians were known as a nation twenty centuries before Christ, and supports his statement by relating that the Armenians went on an expedition against the Phœnicians, a powerful nation at that time; that the Armenians fought and defeated them; and that among the prisoners of war whom they captured was the nephew of Abraham the patriarch. Can any other nation claim such antiquity? It has survived its once-powerful contemporaries, the Assyrians, the Babylonians, the Medians, the Parthians, the Seleucidæ, the Chaldeans, the Egyptians, the Phœnicians, and many other nations of antiquity who now live only in the Classics.

Haiastan, the country of Haik, derived its present name of 'Armenia' from the celebrated ARAM, the sixth successor and lineal descendant of Haik. Aram, who lived 400 years after the patriarch Haik, was a prince of great prowess and skill. He pushed the boundaries of Armenia as far as Asia Minor; defeated the Medes; captured Newkhar, their prince, whom he slew by nailing him through his head to the tower of the fortifications at the royal city of Armavir, where his body was left exposed to public view; and conquered the countries inhabited by the Cappadocians, the Phrygians, and other nations who dwelt in those provinces, whom he forced to adopt, on pain of death, the Armenian language. He carried terror into the neighbouring countries, and gained so much renown and celebrity by his valour and daring deeds that the surrounding nations called the country over which he ruled 'Aramia,' the present name Armenia being a corrupted form.

The first portion of this introductory chapter has been taken up with the origin of the Armenian nation; and as the history of that people would occupy a volume in itself, it will be sufficient to refer to the dynasties which reigned in Armenia during a period of fully 3500 years, from 2111 B.C., when Haik laid the foundation of the Armenian nation, down to the memorable year 1393 A.D., when the Armenians lost their political independence on the death of their last king, Leo VI., of the family of Lusignan. He visited Rome, Spain, England, and France in the vain hope of enlisting the sympathy of Christian Europe, with a view to regaining his throne at Cilicia, from which he had been driven by the Mamelukes of Egypt.* Leo VI. died without male issue at Paris, and his tomb† can be seen at St. Denis, where it was transferred from the Church of the Celestines.

* The dynasty of these once-powerful Mamelukes of Egypt, which gave the death-blow to the political independence of Armenia by the overthrow of the last Armenian kingdom of Cilicia, was founded by slaves. *Mamluc* is the Arabic word for *slave*, and this name was given in Egypt to the slaves of the Beys brought by Saladin II. from the Caucasus, and formed into a standing army. In 1254 A.D. these military slaves revolted; usurped the sovereign power; raised Nour-ud-din Ali, one of their body, to the supreme power of Egypt, and thereby extended their dominions over a great part of Africa, Syria, and Arabia. Nour-ud-din Ali, the founder of the dynasty, was followed by twenty-three successors until the year 1382, when the dynasty of the Borjites, also Mamelukes, succeeded. This second dynasty, after giving twenty-one sultans to Egypt, terminated in 1517, when Egypt was conquered by Selim I., the Sultan of Turkey, who overthrew the Mameluke kingdom, but allowed the twenty-four Beys, the governors of the provinces, to be elected from their body. In 1811, Egypt was conquered by Mohammed Ali, once a humble shopkeeper in an obscure town of Roumelia. He annihilated the turbulent Mamelukes by a wholesale massacre.

† The black marble tombstone, on which is the king's effigy, bears an inscription in French :—"Cy gist le tres noble et tres excellent Prince, Lyon de Lusignan, quint Roi Latin du Royaulme d'Armenie, qui rendit l'ame a Dieu a Paris le XXIX. jour de Novembre, l'an de grace Mccccxciii." It may be rendered into English thus: "Here lieth the noblest and the most excellent Prince, Lyon de Lusignan, the fifth Latin King of the royal house of Armenia, who delivered his soul to God in Paris on the 29th day of November, in the year of grace 1393."

During the long period of 3500 years, only four dynasties reigned in Armenia. Haik, who founded the first dynasty, 2111 B.C., was succeeded by fifty-eight ruling princes: of these, the first forty-one,* although possessing absolute authority, bore the modest title of Prince only. In 752 B.C.—the second year after the foundation of Rome by Romulus,—Armenia, which had hitherto been under patriarchal government, came to be ruled by Paroyr, the forty-second prince of the dynasty. He was an ally of the famous Arbaces, who founded the powerful empire of Media upon the ruins of the Assyrian power, and helped him against Sardanapalus, the effeminate and voluptuous king of Assyria, which resulted in the overthrow of the Assyrian power. Prince Paroyr then assumed the sovereign title, and, in 747 B.C., was publicly crowned king of Armenia: thus for the first time the crown and sceptre, the indispensable insignia of royalty, came to be known and used in Armenia.

It was during the reign of King Paroyr that Adrammelech and Sharezer, fugitive Assyrian princes, sought refuge in Armenia. Having killed Sennacherib, their father, "as he was worshipping in the house of Nisroch, his god," they flew from Nineveh, "and escaped into the land of Armenia" (II Kings xix. 37). There every hospitality was accorded them, and certain portions of land in the south-west of Armenia were allotted to them, where they settled and in course of time formed an important colony. The motive for the patricide was this:—Sennacherib, at the head of a large army, marched against Hezekiah, king

* One of these princes was the warlike Zarmayr, who fought on the side of the Trojans during the Trojan war. After heroically fighting the Greeks during the siege, he fell in an encounter with Achilles, the invulnerable Greek hero of Homeric fame.

of Judah, who had refused to pay him tribute. He entered the country of the Jewish king, and, after taking several fortresses, laid siege to the city of Jerusalem, but his army having been slain at night by the avenging angel of God, he was forced to return to Nineveh.* Thinking that the gods were wroth with him, he resolved upon sacrificing Adrammelech and Sharezer, his sons, who, learning his design, "smote him with the sword" and took to flight.

One of the greatest rulers of this dynasty was King Tigranes I. He reigned forty-five years, from 565 to 520 B.C. As an ally of the famous Cyrus, king of Persia, he accompanied him in his expedition against the kingdom of Assyria, and was present at the taking of the city of Babylon, which was mainly accomplished by the stratagem of deflecting the channel of the Euphrates.† Thereby was fulfilled the prophecy in Jeremiah (li. 27): "Set ye up a standard in the land, blow the trumpet among the nations, prepare the nations against her, call together against her the kingdoms of Ararat, Minni and Ashchenaz; appoint a captain against her; cause the horses to come up as the rough caterpillars."

The first dynasty lasted for 1779 years. It terminated in 332 B.C., when Vahe, the last scion of the House of Haik,

* For a full account of the expedition undertaken by Sennacherib and its total destruction, we would refer our readers to II Kings. chap. xix., and the beautiful lines of Byron on 'The Destruction of Sennacherib.'

† It is related that the troops marched over the former channel of the Euphrates, then dried up, and attacked Babylon by night. Belshazzar, the profligate king of Babylon, who was the grandson of Nebuchadnezzar, was then feasting in his royal palace with his nobles. As they drank wine out of the sacred vessels of the Temple, the fingers of a hand were seen writing on the wall. After the king's soothsayers and astrologers had failed to interpret the writing, the captive Daniel, who was summoned, deciphered and explained it (Dan. v.). Byron, in his 'Vision of Belshazzar,' paints this incident as no other imaginative writer could, perhaps, have done.

fell in battle fighting against Alexander the Great, in attempting to avenge the death of his friend Darius, king of Persia. Darius had been slain by one of his own satraps, Bessus, the governor of Bactriana, while endeavouring to escape after his defeat at Arbela. Armenia then came under the sway of the Macedonian conqueror, and for 176 years was ruled successively by seven Greek Governors. On the death of Alexander in Babylon, on 21st April, 323 B.C., through excessive drinking and debauchery, his vast empire was divided among his generals, when Armenia fell under the power of the Seleucidæ, who governed and held indisputable sway over it until the Parthians appeared in the field as conquerors.

About the year 150 B.C., rose Arsaces the Second, justly styled 'The Great,' who was the grandson of Arsaces the Parthian. He succeeded in shaking off the galling yoke of the powerful Seleucidæ, and, establishing himself king over Parthia, Media, and Babylon, formed them into the powerful Parthian kingdom, to which he subsequently added Armenia. He then expelled Ardavazd, the last Seleucidæ Governor, from Armenia, and appointed his own brother, Vagharshag (Valarsaces), in his place, upon whom he conferred the title of King. Valarsaces thereby became the founder of the second royal dynasty, known as the Arsacidæ, which ruled in Armenia from 149 B.C. to 428 A.D., when Ardashir, the last king of the Arsacidæ, was deposed by Vram, king of Persia, at the instigation of the dissatisfied Armenian chiefs. The dynasty of the Arsacides, which forms a glorious epoch in the history of Armenia, therefore became extinct after having lasted for a period of 577 years.

This dynasty deserves more than a passing notice; for it was during the rule of the powerful Arsacides that the Armenians attained the zenith of their glory and power, and, moreover, gained signal victories over the proud Romans, under their famous king, Tigran II., whom Plutarch and other writers designated 'Tigranes the Great.' This same Tigranes bore the proud title of "King of Kings," he "never appeared in public without having four kings attending him," and, according to Cicero, "made the Republic of Rome tremble before the prowess of his arms."

Tigranes resided at Tigranacerta (the present Diarhekir), at that time the capital of Armenia; and when his brother-in-law, the famous Mithridates, king of Pontus, fled before the Romans, Tigranes afforded him an asylum there. On Tigranes refusing to deliver him up to the Romans, they declared war against him, and marched against Tigranacerta under Lucullus, the celebrated Roman general. The same Lucullus wrote of Tigranes:—

"It is but a few days' journey from the country of the Gabiri or Sebastia [the modern Sivas] into Armenia, where Tigranes, King of Kings, is seated surrounded with that power which has wrested Asia from the Parthians, which carries Grecian colonies into Media, subdues Syria and Palestine."

Rollins, in his *Ancient History*, says:—

"Tigranes, to whom Lucullus had sent an ambassador, though of no great power in the beginning of his reign, had enlarged it so much by a series of successes, of which there are few examples, that he was commonly surnamed 'King of Kings.' After having overthrown and almost ruined the family of the kings, successors of the great Seleucus; after having very often humbled the pride of the Parthians, transported whole cities of Greeks into Media, conquered all Syria and Palestine, and given laws to the Arabians called Scenites, he reigned with an authority respected by all the princes of Asia. The people paid him honours after the manner of the East, even to adoration."

Tigranes the Great reigned in Armenia from 93 B.C. to 39 B.C., and died at the advanced age of eighty-five years. His eventful reign of 54 years furnishes a brilliant page in the history of Armenia.

After the fall of the Arsacidæ dynasty, in 428 A.D., the Sassanidæ of Persia held sway over Armenia until the rise of the Muhammadan power under the Saracens,* who, having invaded Persia in 636 A.D., and overthrown the rule of the Sassanidæ, forced the helpless followers of Zoroaster to embrace the religion of Muhammad. Almost simultaneous with the fall of the Sassanidæ dynasty of Persia, the Saracens, under a chief named Abdur Rahman, invaded Armenia, in 636 A.D. From that time the Caliphs of Damascus and Bagdad held the country until 856 A.D.

During the interregnum between the fall of the second royal dynasty of Armenia, in 428 A.D., and the rise of the third dynasty, in 856 A.D., Armenia was governed by Prefects, appointed at first by the Persians and afterwards by the Caliphs of Damascus and Bagdad respectively. These were selected from among the

---

* Opinions differ as to the origin of the name of *Saracens*, a general appellation given by the Greeks and Latins to the barbaric Arabian tribes who overran the East from the seventh century downwards. According to some writers, the Saracens derived their name from their country—Saracene—part of Arabia Petræa, where they dwelt before they embraced the religion of Muhammad. Ducange, a distinguished French writer and historian, derives this word from *Sarah*, the wife of Abraham the patriarch; Hottinger, from the Arabic *saraca*, to steal; Forster, from *sahra*, a desert; but probably the word is derived from *sharkeyn*, the Arabic word for the eastern people. The name, which, in the middle ages, inspired terror into the hearts of every Christian, was given to any unbaptised person in mediæval romance.

Armenians as well as the Persians. The government of the Prefects, the viceroys of Armenia, terminated in 856 A.D., after having lasted for 428 years.

Their rule forms one of the dark epochs in the history of Armenia, and is memorable for the religious persecutions which the Armenians heroically endured from the Persians and the Arabs for the sake of Christianity. The Armenians—the champions of the Christian faith in the East—rose as one man in 451 A.D., under the leadership of Vardan, the brave Mamigonian chief, to oppose the mighty Persians, who wanted to force upon the Armenians their Zoroastrian religion.*

When the rule of the Prefects ceased, Prince Ashot, an Armenian chief and a scion of the noble house of Bagratoonians, assumed the government of his own tribe, and held at the same time the generalship of the Armenians. Of a patriotic disposition, he evinced great interest in the political and spiritual welfare of his countrymen, and his noble, exemplary character won him the esteem and regard not only of the Armenians, but of the outside world. He found great favour in the eyes of the Caliph of Bagdad, who conferred upon him, in 859 A.D., the entire government of Armenia. Prince Ashot therefore became the founder of the third dynasty in Armenia, known as the Bagratidæ, after the celebrated Bagarad, the ancestor of the family of Bagratoonians, who lived in the days of Valarsaces, the first Arsacide king of Armenia, by whom he was raised to the rank of a nobleman. The Bagratidæ reigned in Armenia for a period of 220 years.

* For an account of this religious war, see the *History of Vartan and of the Battle of the Armenians*, translated by the late Professor C. F. Neumann from the original Armenian text of Elisha, an Armenian writer of great merit in the fifth century, the golden age of Armenian literature.

During that time they had to struggle with the fanatical Saracens on one side, and the Greek emperors of Byzantium (Constantinople) on the other. The capital of the dynasty of the Bagratidæ, founded by Prince Ashot, was the far-famed Ani, and its celebrated ruins at the present day extort the wonder and admiration of the tourist and the archæologist.

After the fall of the third dynasty in Armenia, brought about by the treachery of the Greeks, Rouben, a scion of the family of the Bagratidæ and a relative of Gagik, the last king of that dynasty, whom the Greeks had assassinated, founded, in 1080 A.D., the fourth royal dynasty in far-off Cilicia, where thousands of Armenians had migrated and taken refuge in the fastnesses of the Taurus mountains, flying before the tide of the Mongolian invasion, which had well-nigh devastated their ill-fated fatherland. The dynasty founded by Rouben lasted three centuries. The Armenians had to contend during that period with Muhammadan as well as Christian foes, the latter being the Greeks of Constantinople, whom they defeated on several occasions.

The Crusades commenced during the fourth dynasty, when princes, patricians and plebeians of Christian Europe attempted to wrest the Holy Sepulchre in Jerusalem from the Saracens, the inveterate foes of Christendom. The Armenians of Cilicia rendered yeoman service to the Crusaders, and supplied them with provisions while they laid siege to Antioch. The Crusaders would have endured much greater hardships in their march through Asia Minor *en route* to Palestine, but for the assistance of the Armenians and the protection afforded them by the kings of the Roubenian dynasty, of whom Leo VI. was the last.

From the time Leo VI. was driven from his throne, in 1375 A.D., by the Mamelukes of Egypt, the Armenians have ceased to be an independent nation in the political world. They have, nevertheless, through ages of persecution, tenaciously preserved their nationality by heroically clinging to the Christian faith, which the entire Armenian nation had embraced in the third century by the preaching of St. Gregory of Cæsara, otherwise known as 'Gregory the Illuminator.'

In concluding this chapter, a few interesting extracts, from eminent European writers, with reference to the national characteristics of the Armenian nation and of their wide dispersion over the world, may be found interesting.

Byron, who had a fair knowledge of classical Armenian, and an intimate acquaintance with certain Armenian monks of deep erudition at Venice, wrote in 1817:—

"These men * are the priesthood of an oppressed and a noble nation, which has partaken of the proscription and bondage of the Jews and of the Greeks, without the sullenness of the former or the servility of the latter. This people has attained riches without usury, and all the honours that can be awarded to slavery without intrigue; but they have long occupied, nevertheless, a part of the House of Bondage, who has lately multiplied her many mansions. It would be difficult, perhaps, to find the annals of a nation less stained with crimes than those of the Armenians, whose virtues have been those of peace, and their vices those of compulsion. But whatever may have been their destiny—and it has been bitter,—whatever it may be in future, their country must ever be one

* Byron refers to the Armenian monks of the monastic order of Mekhitar, a religious society of Armenian *literati* with whom the poet tarried while at Venice, where he studied the classical Armenian language—a language so rich, he said, as amply to "repay any one the trouble of learning it."

of the most interesting on the globe; and perhaps their language only requires to be more studied to become more attractive. If the Scriptures are rightly understood, it was in Armenia that Paradise was placed—Armenia, which has paid as dearly as the descendants of Adam for that fleeting participation of its soil in the happiness of him who was created from its dust. It was in Armenia that the Flood first abated and the dove alighted. But with the disappearance of Paradise itself may be dated almost the unhappiness of the country; for, though long a powerful kingdom, it was scarcely ever an independent one, and the satraps of Persia and the pachas of Turkey have alike desolated the region where God created man in His own image."

The Count de Vogue said of them :—

"Lamartine calls the Armenians 'the Swiss of the East.' The term truly describes their probity, their perseverance, their exceptional aptitude for work, and their thrift—qualities which have led to the passage through their hands, in all the commercial centres of the Levant, of at least a third of the moveable capital. These mountaineers, descending from the heights of the Caucasus and the plateau of Van, which was the cradle of their race, have been destined for a wide dispersion. They are perhaps the most striking example of the persistence of a national character, preserved and guaranteed by religion, among the scattered races of the East. Wherever chance has grouped them, they recognize one another, and reunite in communities for mutual alliance and succour, and erect their altar, turning their eyes to the supreme head of their religion, the Patriarch, whose abode is at Etchmiadzine amongst their native mountains. By these special qualities they prove the permanence of the national character which they have inherited."

George Williams, in his *Holy City*, vol. II., p. 556, writes regarding the causes of their wide dispersion :—

"From the fifth century downwards the troubles of Armenia have served to scatter her children over the face of the earth; and the unsettled wandering life, consequent on the absence of a national bond, has served to turn their native spirit of calculation, enterprise, and activity almost exclusively towards commerce, of which they became the principal channels between Europe and Asia. In this view they have established themselves in those places where these two continents come in contact with one another. Under the protection of the Moguls they were scattered throughout the whole of the extensive limits of their settlements in Eastern Europe, in the Khanats of Astrakhan and Khazan, in the Crimea, in the Russian Ukraine, and more especially in Volhynia and Galicia. They followed the footsteps of the Osmarts Turks to Constantinople, and inundated all the eastern coasts of the Mediterranean. The establishment of a Government in the centre of Asia, under the Sophis of Persia, attracted them to the interior of Iran, from whence they penetrated into India, to Madras and Calcutta. In Europe itself they have advanced on one side from the borders of the Austrian kingdom to Venice and Vienna, and on the other from the frontier of the great empire of Russia to Moscow and St. Petersburg. Thus is this nation dispersed over an immense extent of the globe, from the Indian Ocean to the Baltic, from the steppes of Tartary to the valley of the Nile to the crests of the Carpathian Mountains and the Alps, while the land of their fathers is divided between Russia, Turkey, and Persia. Like the Jews, they have retained in all countries their distinctive features and habits, while their general probity has secured for them universal respect."

A writer in the *Christian Remembrancer*, for April 1857, says:—

"Possessing a very distinct nationality, they are found in all towns throughout the Turkish empire, keenly and steadily following trade, and often amassing large fortunes. At Constantinople (including Scutari) there are at least 200,000, some of them men of vast wealth. It was reported that an Armenian, who acted as banker to the Sultan, was worth about thirty millions of English money. They must be the wealthiest community in the Turkish capital. Gradually they are extending themselves throughout Europe; they have long had a monastery, with large printing presses, at Venice; they are found also in Amsterdam and London, and many other centres of commerce: yet in every place they retain their distinct nationality, religion, and language, with an ardent love of their country, and a hope to see it rise to the importance which it once possessed."

The Rev. C. G. Curtis, writing to the *Times*, in 1876, said of them :—

"How much does humanity, how much does Christianity, owe to this race! The Armenians are the only Christian nation in Asia; the Armenian nation was the first to become Christian; missionaries of Christianity in early times, they have been its martyrs in all, from the fifth century, when they rose as one man to repel the Zoroastrians, who tried to force fire-worship into the place of the worship of the true God; through ages of Moslem oppression since, they have passed on an inheritance of resistance and suffering for Christ's sake. It is this nation which seems to be specially marked out to become in time the pioneers of civilization and religion."

In the *Indian Church Quarterly Review* for April 1888, the Rev. Canon Churton writes of the religious fervour of the Armenians :—

"Had it not been for the wonderfully strong hold maintained on this race by its national Church, the nationality of the people must ere this have been lost among the inhabitants of the numerous countries in which they dwell. But so strong a tie has this proved, that although by far the greater number of them are scattered over three quarters of the globe, yet nowhere have they been absorbed, or has their nationality been effaced."

The Armenians in their commercial pursuits are scattered all over the world, and approximately number six millions. Geographically they may be divided thus:—

In Armenia, European and Asiatic Turkey, and Egypt	3,500,000
„ Russia	1,800,000
„ Persia	225,000
„ India, Burmah, the Straits, and Dutch East Indies	25,000
„ Austria-Hungary	25,000
„ Bulgaria, Western Europe, America, &c.	425,000

Having given a brief sketch of the earlier history of the Armenian nation, I shall endeavour to give, in the following chapters, as complete a history as practicable of the Armenians in India, confining myself mainly to remarkable events connected with their early history in the land of their sojourn.

CHAPTER II.

ADVENT OF THE ARMENIANS INTO INDIA.

THE fabulous wealth of India, which from time immemorial had excited the cupidity of many a mighty conqueror and adventurer, also allured many Armenians from their distant homes, around the venerable Ararat, to India's hospitable shores.

From the days of Alexander the Great to the time of Vasco de Gama, who was the first European to reach India by a sea route, while Europe held little or no direct intercourse with the East, Armenians carried on a lucrative trade with this country by the land route *viâ* Persia.

The Armenians, enterprising sons of a noble, but ill-fated, fatherland, although a purely commercial people in India—where they have built no cities, like their *confrères* in trade, the Danes, the Dutch, and the French, —have, however, a history in the land of their sojourn and adoption. It is not, however, one of conquest, adventure, plunder, and rapine, that characterise more or less the policy of other nations which penetrated India, but rather a plain narrative of noteworthy deeds, influenced by strong nationalism and tenacious patriotism, of a handful of Armenian colonists at the various commercial centres of India.

We search in vain the faded pages of Sanskrit writers and Muhammadan chroniclers of ancient times for any reference to this enterprising, commercial people in India. They were hardly interested in politics, and rarely took part in intrigues; their field of action lay, rather, in the bazaars, the commercial marts, and the emporiums of India, over which they exercised vast influence, in the absence of any foreign commercial element, and thereby monopolised the greater portion of the export trade, which they carried on for a considerable period, pouring Indian wares and commodities into Persia and the East on one side, and Venice on the other.

It is interesting, from a historical point of view, to trace in what period of the world's history Armenians first set foot on Indian soil. The writer ventures to assume, after much careful study and antiquarian research, that they were acquainted with India from remote antiquity, *perhaps* even when Semiramis,* the wife of Ninus, and the warlike queen of the once-powerful Assyrian monarchy, reigned supreme in Babylon. Contemporary as a nation with the Assyrians, it is not improbable that they accompanied Semiramis as faithful allies in her invasion of India, which, according to the account given by Ctesias and Diodorus Siculus, was undertaken about the year 2000 B.C., when one Stabrobates (Sthabarpati) held indisputable sway over India of the Vedic times. Armenians, as allies or otherwise, may have accompanied the Greek invasion of India in 327 B.C., under Alexander the Great; for it is a well-known historical fact that he passed through Armenia *en route* for India *viâ* Persia, where he defeated the famous Darius, the Persian king, who resided at Persopolis, the capital of unparalleled architectural fame at that period.

From very early times the Armenians held commercial intercourse with India, where evidently they had

* In the Assyrian inscriptions she is known as Samaraymat.

formed friendly relations with its princes, for policy's sake, and they afforded shelter to two fugitive Indian princes of Kanauj,* who fled their country prior to the Christian era, and sought refuge in far-off Armenia. These fugitive princes, who had conspired against Dinakspall, the Indian king, who reigned supreme at Kanauj, are known in Armenian history by their Hellenised names, 'Gheesaneh' and 'Dimetter,' the former being a corruption of the Indian 'Gonesh' and the latter a literal Greek translation of the Indian 'Juggernath,' which signifies 'the lord of the universe.' It is interesting to follow the history of these Indian refugees, who were received in Armenia, with a welcome befitting, their princely dignity, by Valarsaces, the Armenian king, the younger brother of the great Arsaces, the Parthian, by whom he was appointed king over Armenia about

* Kanauj, a decayed town of historical interest, is situated on the Kalee Nuddee, a river in the district of Farruckabad, which falls into the Ganges three miles below. It lies 52 miles N.-W. from Cawnpore. This once-celebrated town, which, according to the Muhammadan historian Feristha, "contained 30,000 shops for the sale of paun [betel-leaf] and 60,000 families of public dancers and singers," is at present an insignificant place, little more than an expanse of ruins. In its palmy days, according to a learned writer, "the circumvallation covered a space of more than thirty miles." So remote is its antiquity, that some relics of its language, found on coins, &c., baffled the skill of that learned oriental scholar and antiquarian, the late Mr. James Prinsep, in his attempts to decipher them; "the characters," he says, "in which their legends are graven being wholly unknown" This town of ancient India has, not unlike Delhi, experienced great vicissitudes, having been taken successively by the Muhammadan invaders. Mahmood of Ghaznee took the town in 1018, and it was attacked by Shahabuddin Mohammed, sovereign of Ghoor, in 1194, when he defeated Jye Chund Ray, the Hindoo king of Kanauj, and overthrew that monarchy. In 1340 it was taken by the tyrant Mahommed, of the house of Tughlak, who "made an excursion towards Kanauj, and put to death the inhabitants of that city and the neighbourhood for many miles round." It fell into the hands of Baber in 1528, and it was here that Humayon, his son and successor, was defeated, in 1540, by his formidable rival, the Afghan Sher Shah, when he was obliged to fly from Hindustan and seek an asylum at the court of Shah Thamas, the Persian king, who resided at Ispahan, the former capital of Persia.

150 B.C. The Armenian king, their hospitable patron, allotted them the district of Taron, where they built themselves a city, which they styled Veeshap* (Dragon), and afterwards went to the Armenian town of Ashtishat, and there set up their own gods, which they had worshipped in India. After their death these Indian princes were deified by their descendants, who enjoyed the free and undisturbed exercise of their national religion while heathenism was dominant in Armenia. They flourished for a considerable time, and formed an important colony under the auspices of a heathen government, in whose eyes they found favour. The tide of royal kindness, however, began to ebb at the dawn of the Christian faith in idolatrous Armenia in the year 302 A.D., when the Indian shared the fate of the national gods, which were destroyed, and their priests scattered by virtue of a royal edict granted to St. Gregory the Illuminator, the Apostle of Armenia, who converted the whole nation to the Christian faith and rid the land of its idolatry.

In the early part of the Christian era, Kasi, the modern Benares, and at one time the great commercial mart and emporium of India, on the banks of the Ganges, was the head-quarters of the Armenian merchants, who resorted thither from their distant homes by the land route, passing through Persia and Kabul to Benares. The sea route to India *viâ* the Cape of Good Hope was then unknown to European navigators.

Fully seven centuries prior to the landing of Vasco de Gama on the Malabar Coast on that memorable day,

* These princes were of the 'Takshak house,' and they called the city they built in Armenia after their own house. *Takshak* signifies the 'Dragon,' the Armenian name being *Veeshap*.

the 20th of May 1498 A.D., an enterprising Armenian merchant, Mar Thomas by name, had landed on the same coast, in the year 780 A.D., when one Sheo Ram was the native ruler of Cranganore, and in whose eyes he found great favour, which resulted in his amassing considerable riches by trading in muslins and spices, his main object in seeking Indian shores. But the *influx* of Armenians into India dates from the palmy days of the Mogul Empire, the pomp and splendours of whose court (on which the youthful imagination of Milton feasted) drew many an Armenian merchant to Agra, the historical capital of the mighty Moguls, where they formed a commercial settlement.

Akbar the Great adopted the youthful and promising son of a Mr. Jacob, an Armenian merchant, whom he had met at Kashmere during his '*incognito* tours.' This singular adoption was made several years before Jehangeer was born, whose birth in 1570 he attributed to the advent of the Armenians into Agra and their erection, in 1562, of a Christian church there at the express wish of their royal patron. The Armenians flourished in that city during the good old days of the Mogul emperors, with whom they were in the highest favour, of which abundant proofs could be cited.

In the *Journal of the Asiatic Society of Bengal*, vol. lvii., No. I. of 1888 (pt. 1), H. Beveridge, Esq., C.S., discusses at considerable length the works and letters of Father Jerome Xavier, who "is said to have been a native of Navarre in Spain, and a near relative of the great St. Francis [Xavier]. . . . . He came to Goa in 1571. . . . . In 1594 he went on a mission to the emperor Akbar." Mr. Beveridge, in commenting upon a letter written from Akbar's Court in 1598 by Xavier, mentions incidentally:—

"The rest of Xavier's letter is taken up with the account of an *Armenian* who wanted to marry his late wife's niece, and of the danger that the fathers fell into for refusing to celebrate such a marriage."

A church having been built by the Armenians at Agra in 1562, there must have been at least one Armenian priest in spiritual charge of the colony from that time onward. It being contrary to the Armenian church for a man to marry his deceased wife's niece, no Armenian priest could have sanctioned such a marriage; and it is therefore difficult to comprehend what danger the Jesuit fathers incurred in refusing to celebrate that unlawful union. Unfortunately, "the rest of Xavier's letter," which might have elucidated the matter, has not been quoted by Mr. Beveridge.

An interesting episode occurred in connection with the mission of Captain William Hawkins to the Mogul Court at Agra, in the glorious reign of Jehangeer, in whose eyes he found so much favour as almost to border on intimacy. Hawkins arrived at Agra on the 16th April 1609, after encountering many obstacles, and on arrival was sent for by the Emperor. He repaired to the palace and delivered his letter bearing the King's (James I.) seal, which the monarch for some time carefully examined. An old Jesuit acted as interpreter in making known its contents. The Emperor invited Hawkins to visit the palace daily, and held long discourses with him about the different countries in Europe. Jehangeer not only earnestly requested him to remain in India until he could send an embassy to England, but urged him to accept *a wife* in addition to many other donations. This offer Hawkins could not refuse, for policy's sake, but he hoped to evade it by saying that his religious conviction would not allow him to marry anyone but a Christian, thinking that no Christian could be found in that quarter of the globe. But "the Emperor's search was so diligent that he produced *a young Armenian maiden*," whom the Captain married, and they went ultimately to England.

The downfall of the Mogul empire, followed by anarchy and its troublous times, was the death-knell to the commercial pursuits of the Armenians. They deserted the city, and traces of their sojourn are to be seen to this day in the old cemetery of Agra in the shape of tombstones with *Armenian* inscriptions, of which the following are *verbatim* translations:—

> This is the tomb of KHOJAH* MOORAD, who departed to Christ in the year 1645 A.D.
>
> This is the tomb of HAKOB JOHN, son of Khojah Moorad. Died in the year 1657 A.D.
>
> This is the tomb of FRANG, son of Gregory the Mason. Died in the year 1659 A.D.
>
> This is the resting-place of the REVEREND JOHANNESS, son of Johanness Jacob. Died in the year 1668 A.D.
>
> This is the tomb of [*name obliterated*], son of Gregory the Master Mason. Died in the year 1676 A.D
>
> This is the tomb of JOHANNESS MACKERTOOM. Died in the year 1678 A.D.
>
> This is the tomb of the REVEREND ZACHARIAH, from Tabreez, in Persia. Died in the year 1691 A.D.
>
> This is the tomb of the REVEREND BAGDASSAR. Died in the year 1691 A.D.
>
> This is the tomb of HOVAN JOHN, son of Pogose, of the Jrookentz family of Julfa, who died in Christ on the 5th day of Nadar [29th August] in the year 1701 A.D.

These valuable relics and important landmarks of the Armenians at Agra bear silent testimony to their position in the historical capital of the Moguls, concerning which modern Indian historians are silent. The Armenian colonists having built a church at Agra in 1562, many deaths must have occurred previous to 1645, the

* The term 'Khojah' was applied to eminent merchants.

date of the oldest tombstone now to be found there; and it is equally certain that more than nine deaths occurred up to 1701.

In one of his many expeditions against the Turks, who had conquered the greater portion of Armenia, Shah Abbas the Great, king of Persia, had occasion to visit the commercial city of JULFA, on the banks of the Aras river, and a royal reception was accorded him by the opulent citizens. Their wealth dazzled the eyes of this avaricious and crafty monarch, and he resolved to make himself their master. He had long had the development of the trade of his country at heart, and, as there was a lack of commercial enterprise in his own subjects, he determined to make the Armenians, who carried on an extensive and lucrative trade with India, instrumental in improving the trade of his own with other countries, and particularly with India. He carried out his cherished project, to the detriment of the Armenians, whose position as merchants at that period was rather enviable in the commercial world. He issued a mandate to his soldiers, to be carried out *within three days*, that they should raze the town level with the ground and force the inhabitants to leave their homes and migrate to Persia. The hapless Armenians, with tears and lamentations, were thus forced to abandon Julfa, and, after encountering great hardships, about twelve thousand families reached the city of Ispahan in 1605 A.D., where, however, every hospitality was accorded them by the great Shah Abbas. He evinced great interest in his *guests (!)* as he called them, and allotted them an extensive piece of ground in the suburbs of Ispahan on the pleasant banks of the Zenderood. The Armenian colonists there built a city, which they styled NEW JULFA, in everlasting memory of the one abandoned.

New Julfa, the birthplace of the writer, became the important centre of the Persian trade and the head-quarters of the Armenian merchants who poured Indian goods and wares into the Russian and Italian marts by the old caravan route, *viâ* Kabul, Ispahan, Tabreez and Trebizond. This fact accounts for the term 'Persiana,' which the Venetians gave to Indian manufactures, by which name they are called to the present time in the Italian marts. During the halcyon days of Shah Abbas and his worthy successors, the Armenian merchants of New Julfa traded with, but formed no permanent settlements in, India. They returned to New Julfa, built themselves palatial residences on the banks of the Zenderood, and lived like princes. When Shah Abbas and his humane, politic successors passed away, there arose 'a Pharoah who knew not Joseph or his people' (*e.g.*, the Armenians), and persecution and extortion became the order of the day, the opulent Armenian merchants who had rendered such valuable services to that country being the unfortunate victims.

During their commercial pursuits the Armenians had amassed considerable riches and wealth, which roused the cupidity of the Persian monarch of the Nadir Shah type, and he had recourse to tortures of a thrilling nature, with the apparent object of extorting money from them. The result of the persecutions proved disastrous to the trade of the country, for the well-to-do and commercial classes, whose name was legion, fled the country with their families and their wealth, at the dead of night, to avoid detection, like their predecessors the Zoroastrians (the modern Parsees).

From Ispahan they reached Busrah on the Euphrates, and from thence sailed to India. The first port where they formed a permanent settlement in India was the city of Surat. There they erected two churches—one in the city, which is still preserved, but is not now used; the other, which lies in ruins, in their cemetery,—and the extensive cemetery is convincing proof of the flourishing community at that time.

Through their sagacity, they were exceptionally successful in their commercial pursuits, and thereby rose to eminence and found favour in the eyes of the native rulers of Guzerat. Their meridian greatness did not continue long, however, owing to the serious financial misfortunes that befell them during the troublous days of the hostilities between the French and the English in India. The war between these two rival powers in the Carnatic, which broke out in 1783, gave the death-blow to their commercial pursuits in India, and at Surat in particular.* This fact will be seen clearly from the following translation, extracted from an original Armenian letter written from Surat, under date the 28th April 1783, by one Agah Owenjohn Jacob, of the Gerakheantz family, to the Armenian Archbishop of Julfa:—

"We are having troublous times nowadays, as the English are engaged in war with the French and Hyder Ali, and at present they are fighting the Dutch, so that there is war on land and sea. Our [Armenian] merchants lost two lakhs of rupees over a ship from China that was captured at sea, and lately the Maharattas captured a ship bound for Surat from Bengal, whereby we lost two and a half lakhs of rupees."

* I have in my possession a list, in the Armenian language, which comprises the names of 33 Armenian merchants who flourished at Surat during the short space of 20 years, *i.e.*, from 1780-1800, when the following individuals were eminent merchants:—Agah Owenjohn Jacob of the Gerakheantz family of Julfa, Agah Mackertich Melikhnazean, Agah Gaspar Johanness, and Agah George Ter Arratoon. The term 'Agah,' like 'Khojah,' was applied to merchants of eminence.

The same letter, after giving a minute account of a severe storm that had raged at Surat in the previous month, goes on to say:—

"A ship bound for Busrah was lost at sea, in which our [Armenian] merchants lost goods worth one and a half lakhs. From Bombay the Armenians had sent us a consignment of forty-two bales of silk, but the ship was wrecked and the cargo lost. All these misfortunes befell us within the space of forty days: we are at a loss what to do. The entire loss sustained by our merchants at Surat alone amounts to more than six lakhs, of which the major portion belonged to me. God's will be done."

Writing on 18th February 1784, or about nine months after the previous letter, he wrote to the following effect, of which this is a translation:—

"We are gradually declining and getting poorer, and dangers and calamities are on the increase daily. Many sustained heavy losses and became bankrupt owing to the severe storm that raged in March last, in which I alone lost Rs. 56,000. At present the Java ships are being either captured or wrecked at sea, whereby our merchants have already lost two lakhs of rupees, of which Rs. 13,000 belonged to me."

I have in my possession an autograph letter, written from Surat by one Johanness Seth (connected with our family), dated 28th February 1797, to my great-grandfather at Julfa, Ispahan, of which the following extract is a translation:—

"You ask me earnestly with regard to our brother Seth's voyage, the details of which he has not written you, but which are, however, as follow:—Agah Marooth, my principal, had purchased a ship and named it *Arshak*, in which he loaded goods to the extent of Rs. 1,50,000 for export. He appointed Mr. Seth as super-cargo and gave him Rs. 8,000 as his share in the concern. He also gave him goods worth Rs. 20,000 for sale at Malacca,* and others had given goods for Rs. 15,000. Mr. Seth himself had invested *his all* in goods and loaded in the same ship of which he was the super-cargo. He started with others in the *Arshak* and safely reached Madras, and sailing from thence arrived in safety at Penang. There they sold a considerable portion of their goods, and after making further purchases embarked for Malacca. While at sea and within a short distance of Malacca, they were attacked by three French frigates, who opened fire and captured them. After plundering them of all they possessed, the French put them ashore at Penang, from whence they returned to Surat deprived of all they possessed. This disastrous event was a source of great financial loss first to Agah Marooth, secondly to me, and last, though not least, to our poor brother, Mr. Seth,† who thereby *lost all that he possessed*, and for which he had toiled for so many years. Under the circumstances, his loss is keenly felt by us. All these, our present misfortunes, are mainly due to the wars that are being waged

---

* Malacca was captured by the Portuguese, under Albuquerqe, in 1509, when Portugal was a great maritime power and had command over the eastern seas. It fell afterwards into the hands of their rivals, the Dutch, in 1642. They, in their turn, were expelled by the English in 1795. who retain Malacca to the present day. It was a town of considerable importance both from a political and commercial point of view, owing to its favourable situation. Commerce, that had given significance to the place, had allured thither Armenian merchants from India and elsewhere. There they formed a settlement and built for themselves a National Church. Traces of their sojourn are to be seen to this day in the shape of tombstones inscribed in Armenian. The following is a translation of one of these rare and interesting inscriptions, of which I have a copy in my possession :—

"Hail thou that readst the tablet of my tomb! wherein I now do sleep :
Give me the news, the freedom of my countrymen, for them I did much weep ;
If there arose amongst them one good guardian to govern and to keep.
Vainly I expected in the world to see a good shepherd come to look after the scattered sheep :
I, Jacob, the grandson of Shameer, an Armenian of a respectable family whose name I keep,
Was born in a foreign place in Persia in new Julfa, where my parents now for ever sleep ;
Fortune brought me to this distant *Malacca*, which my remains in bondage doth keep.
Separated from the world on the 7th July in the year of our Lord 1774 at the age of 29.
And my mortal remains were deposited in this spot, in the ground which I had purchased.'

† The unfortunate Mr. Seth referred to was the grandfather of the writer. He died at Bushire in 1822, while on a visit from Julfa, Ispahan.

between the English and the French and other European nations, for which we, as well as merchants of other nationalities, have suffered heavily during these few years. I may add that, in the present year alone, the merchants in the Fort here have lost fifteen lakhs of rupees. It is the same all over India. There is no more life in us. May God have mercy on our merchants, whose affairs are by no means in a healthy condition!"

In the *Calcutta Review* for March 1848, there is an interesting article on 'Surat: Its Past and Present,' from which the following, connected with the history of Armenians there, is an extract:—

"Previous to the decline of the Mogul empire, the city was under a Governor, to whom the Cutwal was subordinate. There was also a Governor of the Castle, the two Governors being perfectly independent of each other, and solely responsible to the Emperor, who reserved to himself the power of life and death, and to whom reference was made before the infliction of capital punishment. There was a strict police surveillance, but the functionaries were, like other orientals, accessible to bribes. The Cutwal himself was obliged to parade the streets during the night, and persons found in them were ordinarily imprisoned. Guards were placed at various stations, and at nine, twelve, and three o'clock the Cutwal passed with tom-toms, horns, and the shouts of his attendants, who were answered by the detached police. An incident, however, which occurred during Thevenot's* stay, proves that all this was little more than an organized system of tyranny. A certain Armenian merchant had been robbed of two thousand four hundred sequins; at the same time two of his slaves disappeared and were suspected of the theft. After strict enquiry had been made, and neither money nor slaves discovered, a report gained ground that the slaves had committed the theft, that they had been drawn to the house of a

* The author of *Le Voyage de M. De Thevenot.*

certain Mussalman with whom they were in communication, and were murdered by him for the sake of the stolen property. The Governor urged upon the Cutwal the necessity of making good the Armenian's loss, for, if a report were sent to the Emperor, all blame would fall upon him. The Cutwal did not object, but simply demanded that they would wait a short time, until he might place the merchant and his servants under restraint and examine the latter by torture. The Governor consented; but, as soon as the Armenian was informed of the new turn which affairs had taken, he let the prosecution drop, and preferred losing the whole of his money to suffering the tortures which the Cutwal had in store for him."

The same article goes on to say:—

"There are about twenty Armenians with their priest [at Surat]. We know not how to account for the large proportion of women amongst them, but such there is; and when a report of the population of Surat was sent to England in 1824, the case was precisely the same, although in all other instances the numbers of males and females were about equal. The occupation of these once-active people is almost gone. No greater testimony could have been given to their industry, honesty, and ability, than the circumstance that they were employed by our factories to carry on their trade in the interior, the Company admitting that they could conduct it better than their own agents. In their altered position they still retain the respectability and love of order for which they are generally so distinguished."

With the following sad, but interesting, incident this rather lengthy notice of the Armenian colony at Surat will conclude. An Armenian jeweller arrived at Surat from Busrah, and hired a room in the immediate vicinity of the Armenian Church. He dealt in precious stones with men of all nations, and one day the legal adviser to the Governor of Surat paid him a visit, on the pretext of buying stones for the Governor. On finding the Armenian jeweller alone, his cupidity was aroused, and he stabbed him. After taking all his valuable goods, he took to his heels and made himself scarce. Two days afterwards, which was a Sunday, and the Armenians not seeing him at church as usual, they became anxious about him. On going to his room, they found the body of the jeweller lying prostrate on the floor, stabbed in the region of the heart. After a careful search, the murderer was arrested with the stones in his possession. The Armenians of Surat demanded justice from the Governor for the atrocity perpetrated on their fellow-countryman, but were told by him that "for the life of an Armenian *even the point of the nail* of the legal adviser would not be cut." According to popularly-accepted tradition amongst the Armenians in India, his doom was thereby sealed, as the English, who were waiting for a favourable moment to take Surat, availed themselves of this opportunity, and came and made themselves masters of the city, where the first English factory in India was established in 1612 by permission of Jehangeer, the great Mogul Emperor.

CHAPTER III.

LANDMARKS OF ARMENIANS IN BEHAR AND BENGAL.

THE Armenians had formed some commercial settlements in Bengal prior to the advent of the English settlers. From Benares and Patna they had journeyed eastwards and settled in the commercial centres of Bengal, which was a dependency of the Mogul empire in those days. Armenians had also lived and died at the town of Behar, the ancient Magadha. Two tombstones, with Armenian inscriptions, now in the Indian Museum at Calcutta, were brought from Behar by the Bengal Archæological Department, and thus saved from inevitable oblivion. The inscriptions may thus be rendered into English :—

No. 1.—"This is the tomb of MARGAREH, son of Avietick, of the Khastatentz family. Died in the year 1646 A.D."

No. 2.—"This is the tomb of MIRZAKHAN . . . . ?, who was a native of Julfa. Died in the year 1693 A.D."

They are to be seen in the gallery specially devoted to Epigraphy in the Museum, and are referred to in vol. i., page 38, of the Archæological Survey Reports. Other valuable landmarks of the history of the Armenians in Behar are still to be found at that station.

Inscription No. 1 is comparatively in a fair state of preservation, in spite of its having been exposed to the effects of the Indian sun and rain for about two hundred anb fifty years. The ruthless hand of Time has not, however, so carefully guarded the inscription on the other tombstone, but happily the *year* is preserved, which is of the first archæological importance. I have, nevertheless, succeeded in deciphering the Christian name upon it, but the family name is practically undecipherable. It is known, however, that his name was Mirzakhan, that he was a native of Julfa in Ispahan, and that he died in Behar in the year 1693, when the Armenians were great traders in Behar, Patna, and Benares, from whence they moved eastward, and ultimately came and settled in Bengal—'The Paradise of Nations,' as emphatically characterised by the Emperor Aurungzebe—in the palmy days of Muhammadan sway.

Armenians, the pioneers of the early foreign traders in India, and the most enterprising commercial community from the remotest times, formed their *first* settlement in Bengal during the halcyon days of the Mogul supremacy, when the far-famed and historical court at Murshidabad, the seat of the Mogul viceroys of Bengal, was at the zenith of its glory, but which eventually dwindled away and sank into insignificance under impolitic viceroys and rash nawabs of the Suraj-ud-Dowlah type. The Armenians formed a permanent settlement at Syedabad, the commercial suburb of Murshidabad, by virtue of a *royal firman* issued in 1665 by Aurungzebe, the Mogul Emperor of Delhi, granting them a piece of land at that place, with full permission to form a settlement there. The Armenians flourished at Syedabad for a considerable time, but finally deserted it, in the natural course of events, when it lost its commercial importance. The only traces now left of that once-flourishing community are the Armenian church and a number of tombstones with Armenian inscriptions.

At Syedabad the Armenians rendered valuable services to the Hon'ble East India Company during the eventful year 1756, when Holwell and his fellow-captives were taken to Murshidabad after the tragedy of the historical

Black Hole of Calcutta. The Armenian inhabitants of Syedabad, and Agah Manuel Satoor in particular, treated the hapless captives with much kindness, sympathising with them as fellow-Christians in a foreign land.

Regarding the settlements of the Armenians in Bengal, Bolts remarks, in his work already referred to :—

"The Armenians, who have ever been a great commercial body in Hindustan, have also long had considerable settlements in Bengal, particularly at Syedabad. Their commerce was likewise established by the Mogul's *firman*, whereby the duties on the two principal articles of their trade, piece-goods and raw silk, were fixed at three-and-a-half per cent."

The Dutch, who had traded with India before the advent of the English, and who were in many respects their rivals in those days, showing as much energy in war as in trade, had formed in 1652 an important commercial settlement at Chinsurah (the Cheechrah of the Armenians), a suburb two miles to the south of the old city of Hooghly. In 1826, Chinsurah was ceded to the English by the Dutch in exchange for Sumatra, after they had held it for about two centuries. Hooghly has acquired some celebrity in connection with the Roman Catholic church and priory at Bandel, being the *oldest Christian church in Bengal.* It was erected by the Portuguese in 1599, burnt down by the Moguls in 1632 during the siege of Hooghly, and rebuilt shortly after by its followers.

The Armenians, who traded largely and were influential politicians in the days of the Mogul supremacy, attached themselves to their *confrères* in trade, the Dutch, at Chinsurah in the year 1645, under the leadership of the famous and opulent Margar family, who were high in the favour of kings and their viceroys.

The Armenian church at Chinsurah, acknowledged to be the *second oldest Christian church in Bengal*, was erected by this pious Margar family. In 1695 they laid the foundations of a national church at Chinsurah, which was completed in 1697, and dedicated to St. John the Baptist. Its splendid steeple, which serves as a belfry, was erected in the early part of the present century by Sophia Simon Bagram, a pious Armenian lady of Calcutta.

The most prominent member of the noble Margar family was the famous Khojah Johanness Margar, who died in 1697. His tomb is to be seen to this day in the churchyard of Chinsurah. It bears an interesting inscription in Armenian verse, of which the following is a translation :—

"This is the tomb wherein lies interred the famous Kharib [*i.e.*, Foreigner] KHOJAH JOHANNESS, the son of Margar, an Armenian from Julfa, in the country of Shosh. He was a considerable merchant, honoured with the favours of kings and of their viceroys [governors]. He was handsome and amiable, and had travelled north, south, east, and west, and died suddenly at the City of Hooghly, in Hindustan, on the 27th November 1697, and delivered up his soul into the hands of the angel and rested here in a foreign land in solicitude of a house [home]. The end of the world will come, the [glory of the] Cross will dawn in the East, the trumpet of Gabriel will be blown suddenly at the middle of the night, the judgment-seat will be set up for the Bridegroom to come and sit thereon, [and who will say] 'Come ye, the blessed of the heavenly Father.' And may He deem him [Khojah Johanness] worthy, like the five wise virgins, to be in readiness to enter into the sacred pavilion [the nuptial chamber] which only the righteous inherit on the right [side] of the saints.

"Oh ye, who may come across this tomb, pray for him earnestly, and may God have mercy on your parents and *on me*, the Rev. Gregory,* who am a native of Erivan. Here endeth the inscription :—

"VIIAZIOAO MARCOS ARMENIODANUS.

"Sad Sño. 1697."

* The composition of the above inscription in the original Armenian is that of the Rev. Gregory. In olden times, this task generally devolved upon the priests.

Chinsurah was also deserted by the Armenians on losing its commercial importance, and the only trace that is left there of the once-flourishing Armenian community is the national church of St. John the Baptist, where the pious Margar family sleep.

The Chinsurah church has not, however, shared the fate of the Armenian church at Syedabad, where "the sweet sound of the church-going bell is never heard," and the walls of which no more redound with the melodious songs and devotional chants of its ministers and congregation.

Divine service is frequently held on Sundays at the Chinsurah Armenian church, and is served by one of the three ministers attached to the Armenian church of Calcutta. It is a time-honoured custom with the Armenian community of Calcutta to attend divine service *annually* at that church on the anniversary of the Feast of St. John the Baptist, the patron saint, which regularly falls on the 26th day of January. It is celebrated by great solemnity and devotion, when service of the Holy Mass is held. On that occasion the Armenians attend divine service with as much zeal and devotion as the Roman Catholics at the Bandel church on the festival of the Novena, which is celebrated by them in November, and to which a great number of Roman Catholics then resort.

CHAPTER IV.

ARMENIANS AND THE EAST INDIA COMPANY.

A VERY valuable discovery, relating to the early history of the Armenian settlement of Calcutta, was made under auspicious circumstances. In October 1894, I was requested by the Bengal Government to translate into English a number of classical Armenian inscriptions in the Armenian churchyards at Syedabad and Chinsurah, and last, though not least, in the churchyard of St. Nazareth at Calcutta, in connection with a valuable list of inscriptions on the Christian tombs and monuments in Bengal possessing historical or archæological interest, which is nearly ready for publication by the Bengal Government. I undertook the work merely for the love of it; and, though arduous, it soon became a source of great pleasure, as it stimulated my antiquarian proclivities, which had until then been practically dormant.

During one of these antiquarian researches in the Armenian churchyard, I came across a vein of gold—a veritable stream of Pactolus,—the interesting inscription referred to above, the discovery of which, being *the oldest* in Calcutta, has excited considerable curiosity. Those interested in ANTIQUE CALCUTTA, and antiquarians enthusiastic in the early history of the present metropolis, with its queer reminiscences and deeply interesting historical associations, have been surprised by the revelation that there exists in the Calcutta Armenian churchyard *a much older Christian tomb* than that of Job Charnock in the churchyard of St. John's Church (the old Cathedral), whose shrine, according to the popularly-accepted tradition in connection with the founding of Calcutta by him, in 1690, was hitherto acknowledged as the oldest in Calcutta.

Prior to the days of Job Charnock and his founding of Calcutta in 1690, the Armenians, whose love of commerce has always been proverbial, had formed a small commercial settlement in the village of Sutanati, corresponding with the native portion of Calcutta traversed by Chitpore Road. Hautkola Ghât was then known as *Sutanati* Ghât. Though this statement regarding the early settlement of the Armenians in Calcutta might be questioned by zealous critics and antiquarians, it is supported by monumental evidence which places its accuracy beyond all doubt. The writer has lately brought to light an interesting inscription, in the Armenian language, on a tombstone in the Armenian churchyard of Calcutta, bearing date the 11th July 1630 A.D., of which the following is a verbatim translation :—

"This is the tomb of REZABEEBEH, wife of the late charitable Sookeas, who departed from this world to life eternal on the 21st day of Nakha [11th July] in the year 15 [New Era of Julfa*= 1630 A.D.]."

That the Armenians had established themselves in Calcutta before the arrival of Job Charnock, is evident from the date of the above inscription, which is beyond doubt the oldest in Calcutta. The authenticity of the date might be questioned on the ground that the present Armenian church was not at that time in existence,

* The New Era of Julfa in this year of grace (1895) is 280, and is known amongst us as the 'Era of Azarea,' after one Azarea who reformed the Calendar. This era dates from the founding of the city of Julfa, a suburb of Ispahan and the headquarters of Armenians in Persia, where they have settled since the days of Shah Abbas the Great, in the early part of the seventeenth century.

having been erected in the year 1724. Its site was the old Armenian burying-ground: it is referred to in a subsequent chapter. Previous to 1724 the Armenians worshipped in a small chapel, built of timber, about a hundred yards to the south of the present church.

This Armenian inscription upsets the ordinarily-accepted account of the history of Calcutta prior to the British settlement, for it dates as far back as 1630, or about sixty years before Job Charnock, the East India Company's Agent, set foot in Calcutta and hoisted the British Flag on the banks of the Hooghly on that memorable day, the 24th of August 1690. The discovery has been hailed with enthusiasm by scholars and antiquarians of note, as will be seen from the following leading article, printed *in extenso*, which appeared in the *Englishman* (Calcutta), on 31st January 1895, under the heading, 'Armenian Founders of Calcutta':—

"It is gratifying to learn that the efforts which have recently been made by various enquirers and in various ways to push back the history of Calcutta to the remoter past, before the formation of the English settlement under Job Charnock, have not been altogether without fruit. By slow degrees evidences are being accumulated which tend to connect Calcutta with earlier traders and to prove that even before the building of Fort William the place was not without importance. Among such evidences one of the most striking is the discovery which has been recently made by Mr. M. J. Seth, an enthusiastic Armenian scholar, who, at the instance of Government, has translated a large number of the classical Armenian inscriptions in the churchyard of St. Nazareth, Calcutta. The earliest inscription runs as follows:—

"'This is the tomb of REZABEEBEH, the wife of the late charitable Sookeas, who departed from this world to life eternal on the 21st day of Nakha in the year 15,' "that is, on the 11th July 1630 A.D. What a world of questions is suggested by this newly-found record! Why was this source of information never utilised before? Who was the 'charitable Sookeas,' and how did his family come to be living in Calcutta sixty years before the advent of the English? Was there already an Armenian settlement here? Are the Armenians, after all, the founders of the city?

"Upon these questions our early records do not cast much light, but they supply other equally important information about the Armenians in Calcutta. If they do not enable us to decide whether there was an Armenian colony settled here before 1690, they show that it was through the Armenians that the English colony secured a footing in the country. If Job Charnock be the founder of Calcutta, the author of its privileges and early security is the great Armenian merchant, Khojah Israel Sarhad. In a recent article we mentioned this remarkable man as one of the embassy sent to Delhi in 1715; such a bare notice does but scanty justice to the services which he rendered on that occasion, and not on that occasion only, but at a still earlier period, when the English were even more in need of help. It is at the time of the rebellion of Subha Singh, when the English were just beginning to build their fort, that 'Cojah Surhaud,' as he is called, first appears in the records. In June 1687 he was sent as Political Agent to the camp of Zabardast Khan, the Mogul General engaged in suppressing the revolt. Here, however, he met with no success till at the end of the year Azim-ush-Shan arrived in Bengal and assumed command. At the court of this easy-going Prince, Sarhad succeeded in ingratiating himself by his prudent conduct and winning address, and in particular in becoming a prime favourite with Azim-ush-Shan's young son, Furrukh Siyar, then about fourteen years old. The friendship of the future Emperor was won by 'presents of toys, at that time very acceptable, for which he expressed a great deal of satisfaction, often sending for Cojah Surhaud and making him sit by him many hours to show what uses they were for.' The result of this judicious management was that, in July 1698, for the sum of sixteen thousand rupees the English acquired letters-patent from the Prince, allowing them to purchase from the existing holders the right of renting the three villages of Calcutta, Sutanati, and Govindpur.

"After this remarkable achievement, Khojah Sarhad drops out of sight for some time. He was apparently more successful as a Political Agent than as a merchant. As early as 1707 we find that he owed the Company considerable sums of money, which he could not pay. At the beginning of 1713 the debts amounted to Rs. 38,831-2-0, and it became necessary for the English Council to take up the matter seriously. Sarhad explained that he had enough and more than enough to pay the debts in Goa. In 1710 he had consigned to his factor there, one Avenoose, goods to the value of Rs. 75,000; but Avenoose was dead, and his successor, Aga Peerie, had made no returns. The Council, therefore, sent a sloop under Captain Delaforce to secure Sarhad's property, and wrote letters to the Portuguese Viceroy of Goa and the English Agent at Calicut, asking for their assistance. It is disappointing to have to add that the records tell us nothing more about this business, but we may safely assume that it terminated satisfactorily. At any rate, in this same year (1713), Sarhad comes to notice again as a negotiator. The English were now bent on sending off their embassy to Furrukh Siyar, now Emperor at Delhi, and his quondam playfellow was of the greatest use in arranging the preliminaries. Through another Armenian, Khojah Manur, who was then in attendance on the Padishah Begam, the daughter of Aurangzebe, he 'prevailed with the King to order a *hasb-ul-hukum** to be given, ordering all *subahs*, governors, and officers whatsoever to guard our present

* The *hasb-ul-hukum* was an official confirmation, under the seal of the *wazir*, enforcing obedience to the Emperor's *firman*.

for the King through their several Governments till it shall arrive, with the English that shall accompany it and Cojah Surhaud at Court.' It is not surprising, therefore, that, when the present was at length sent off, Sarhad was made second in the management of the embassy. On the 5th of June 1714, 'it was unanimously agreed that Cojah Surhaud, whose interest, etc., at Court has already had the good effect of procuring us the *hasb-ul-hukum* and several other useful orders from Court, be sent to assist in suing for the King's *firman*, and that he sit and vote in the Council along with the three English gentlemen.' 'It is absolutely necessary,' adds the record book, 'that some person who is perfect master of the Persian language and understands our affairs very well, and what may be useful for us be sent, and we know no man so qualified in both these respects as Cojah Surhaud. He is, therefore, the fittest man to send.' The event, as is well known, justified this selection. The English embassy, aided partly by the favourable impression produced by the skill of Dr. Hamilton, and still more by the diplomatic talents of Khojah Sarhad, procured from Furrukh Siyar a number of privileges which, though never realised to their full extent, were yet sufficient to keep Calcutta and its trade safe from molestation till the days of Suraj-ud-Dowlah."

Job Charnock, whose name will be handed down to posterity as the founder of the present 'City of Palaces,' died on the 10th day of January 1692 A.D. (*decimo die Januarii 1692*), according to the Latin inscription on his tombstone in the Charnock mausoleum in St. John's churchyard, which was the old burying-ground of the English settlement prior to the re-erection of the present church in 1784, the previous one having been destroyed, in the eventful year 1756, by the fiendish tyrant Nawab Suraj-ud-Dowlah. The inscription on his tombstone runs as follows:—

"D. O. M. JOBUS CHARNOCK, Armiger, Anglus, et nup in hoc Regno Bengalensi, dignissimus Anglorum Agens. Mortalitatis suæ exuvias sub hoc marmore deposuit, ut in spe beatæ resurrectionis ad Christi Judicis adventum obdormirent. Qui post quam in solo non suo peregrinatus esset diu, reversus est domum suæ æternitatis decimo die Januarii 1692."

It may thus be translated:—

"To the great and good God! Job Charnock, Esq., Englishman, and lately in this Kingdom of Bengal, a most worthy Agent of the English, laid down the remains of his mortality under this marble monument that they might sleep in the hope of a blessed resurrection at the coming of Christ the Judge. After he had sojourned for a long time in a land not his own, he returned to his eternal home on the 10th day of January 1692."

I must here ask the reader's indulgence for an interesting digression, regarding the early settlement of the English in Calcutta under Job Charnock.

Captain Alexander Hamilton, who spent his time in the East Indies, from 1688 to 1723, in "trading and travelling by sea and land between the Cape of Good Hope and the Island Japan," gives the following particulars:—

"The English settled at Calcutta about the year 1690, after the Mogul had pardoned all the robberies and murders committed on his subjects. Mr. Job Channock [Charnock] being then the Company's Agent in Bengal, he had the liberty to settle an emporium in any part on the river's side below Hughly, and, for the sake of a large shady tree, chose to that place, though he could not have chosen a more unhealthy place on all the river; for three miles to the north-eastward is a salt-water lake that overflows in September and October, and then prodigious numbers of fish resort thither, but in November and December, when the floods are dissipated, those fishes are left dry, and with their putrefaction affect the air with thick stinking vapours, which the north-east winds bring with them to Fort William, that they cause a yearly mortality. One year I was there [this must have been soon after 1706], and there were reckoned in August about 1,200 English, some military, and some servants to the Company, some private merchants residing in the town, and some seamen belonging to the shipping lying at the town, and before the beginning of January there were four hundred and sixty burials registered in the Clerk's Book of Mortality.

"Mr. Charnock, choosing the ground of the colony where it now is, reigned more absolute than a rajah, only he wanted much of their humanity; for when any poor, ignorant natives transgressed his laws, they were sure to undergo a severe whipping for a penalty, and the execution was generally done when he was at dinner, so near his dining room that the groans and cries of the poor delinquents served him for music.

"The country about being overspread with Paganism, the custom of wives burning with their deceased husbands is also practised here. Before the Mogul's war, Mr. Charnock went one time with his ordinary guard of soldiers to see a young widow act that tragical catastrophe, but he was so smitten with the widow's beauty, that he sent his guards to take her by force from the executioners, and conduct her to his own lodgings. They lived lovingly many years, and had several children; at length she died, after he had settled in Calcutta, but, instead of converting her to Christianity, she made him a proselyte to Paganism, and the only part of Christianity that was remarkable in him was burying her decently, and he built a tomb over her, where all his life after her death he kept the anniversary-day of her death by sacrificing a cock on her tomb, after the Pagan manner. This was, and is, the common report, and I have been credibly informed, both by Christians and Pagans, who lived at Calcutta under his Agency, that his story was really true matter of fact."

The insanitary condition of old Calcutta is also depicted in the following poem by Atkinson, on 'The City of Palaces'—which was 'a veritable Golgotha,' as it was sometimes called:—

"Calcutta! What was thy condition then?
An anxious, forced existence, and thy site
Embowering jungle, and noxious fen,
Fatal to many a bold aspiring wight:
On every side tall trees shut out the sight;
And like the Upas, noisome vapours shed;
Day blazed with heat intense, and murky night
Brought damps excessive and a feverish bed:
The revellers at eve were in the morning dead.

Worse than Batavia, thou wert then a tomb
What art thou now, amidst thy various brood?
Though unincumbered by a forest's gloom,
Thou robbest beauty of its eloquent blood,
Youth of its lustre, and the opening bud
Of infancy is blasted in thy view;
Fell as the Vampire in its thirstiest mood,
All ranks alike thy direful influence rue,
Thou bane of lovely looks and health's inspiring hue."

Raikes, in his *Englishman in India*, writes:—

"He [Charnock] retained a sergeant as a bully, and allowed the secretary and captain of soldiers to keep a punch-house and billiard-table, and to send in false returns to his employers, in aid of the tavern funds. The Home Government, until the days when all their attention was absorbed by jealousy of rival trading associations, did what they could to restrain the licentiousness of their servants abroad, remarking that the disorderly conduct of their factors tended to the dishonour of God, the discredit of the Gospel of our Lord, and the shame and scandal of the English nation. They sent out strict rules for the conduct of their subordinates, and directed that hardened offenders should be at once sent home. They also directed the use of a form of prayer, beseeching God that 'these Indian nations, amongst whom we dwell, seeing our sober and righteous conversation, may be induced to have a just esteem for our most holy profession of the Gospel.'"

According to Orme, the historian,

"Charnock was a man of courage, without military experience, but impatient to take revenge on a Government [the Mogul] from whom he had personally received the most ignominious treatment, having been imprisoned and scourged by the Nabob."

When Job Charnock founded Calcutta, in 1690, he invited the Armenians, and the Portuguese at Chinsurah, to his new factory. The former accepted his invitation, and placed themselves under the protection of the English traders, to whom they rendered invaluable services on various occasions, as will be seen in the course of this work.

The first account of the connection of the Armenians in India with the Hon'ble East India Company, which represented the British Nation in this country, is found in vol. iii. of *Considerations on Indian Affairs*, by W. Bolts, published in London in 1782. The Armenians attached themselves to the English in 1688, through their representative, the well-known Khojah Phanoos Khalanthar, an Armenian of renown and great influence, who was a native of Julfa, in Ispahan. As a result of the negotiations between "The Governor and Company of Merchants of London trading to the East Indies" and the Armenians in India, through their representative, Khojah Phanoos Khalanthar (Cazee Phanoos Calendar), "a merchant of eminency," as he is styled by the East India Company, the Hon'ble the Court of Directors, on entering into an agreement with the Armenians, issued the following 'Charters' under date the 22nd of June 1688 :—

"THE GOVERNOR AND COMPANY OF MERCHANTS OF LONDON trading to the East Indies, to all to whom these presents shall come, send greeting.

"Whereas representation hath been made to us by Sir Josiah Child, Baronet, our Deputy-Governor, that, upon long conferences by him had with Cazee [Khojah]

Phanoos Calendar [Khalanthar], an Armenian merchant of eminency, and an inhabitant of Ispahan, in Persia, as also with Sir John Chardin of London, Knight, they had, on behalf of the Armenian nation, proposed to him several particulars for carrying on a great part of the Armenian trade to India and Persia, and thence to Europe, by way of England, which will redound greatly to His Majesty's advantage in his customs and to the increase of the English navigation, if the Armenian nation might obtain such license from this Company as will give them encouragement to alter and invert the ancient course of their trade to and from Europe. And we being always willing to increase and encourage the public trade and navigation of this kingdom, after a serious debate of all the propositions relating to this affair, have thought fit to agree and resolve as follows, *viz.*:—

"'*First.* That the Armenians shall now, *and at all times hereafter*, have equal share and benefit of all indulgences this Company have or shall at any time hereafter grant to any of their own adventurers or other English merchants whatsoever.

"'*Secondly.* That they shall have free liberty at all times hereafter to pass and repass to and from India in any of the Company's ships on as advantageous terms as any free man whatsoever.

"'*Thirdly.* That they shall have liberty to live in any of the Company's cities, garrisons, or towns in India, and to buy, sell, and purchase land and houses, and be capable of all civil offices and preferments in the same manner as if they were Englishmen born, and shall *always* have the free and undisturbed liberty of the exercise of their own religion. And we hereby declare that we will not continue any Governor in our service that shall in any kind disturb or discountenance them in the full enjoyment of all the privileges hereby granted to them, neither shall they pay any other or greater duty in India than the Company's factors, or any other Englishmen born, do, or ought to do.

"'*Fourthly.* That they may voyage from any of the Company's garrisons to any other ports or places in India, the South Seas, China or the Manillas, in any of the Company's ships, or any permissive free ships allowed by the Company, and may have liberty to trade to China, the Manillas or any other ports or places within the limits of the Company's Charter upon equal terms, duties and freights with any free Englishman whatsoever,'" &c., &c.

The rest of the agreement refers to the import duties on various classes of goods.

Simultaneously with the above, another Charter was granted to the Armenians, which ran as follows :—

"Whenever forty or more of the Armenian nation shall become inhabitants of any garrison cities, or towns, belonging to the Company in the East Indies, the said Armenians shall not only enjoy the free use and exercise of their religion, but there shall also be allotted to them a parcel of ground to erect a church thereon for worship and service of God in their own way. And that we also will, at our own charge, cause a convenient church to be built of timber, which afterwards the said Armenians may alter and build with stone or other solid materials to their own good liking. And the said Governor and Company will also allow fifty pounds per annum, during the space of seven years, for the maintenance of such priest or minister as they shall choose to officiate therein. Given under the Company's larger seal, June 22nd, 1688."

As a mark of their esteem and appreciation for Khojah Phanoos Khalanthar, the Court of Directors conferred upon him a personal privilege, granting him, by a separate Charter on the same date, the sole monopoly of the trade in 'Garnet' and 'Amethyst' stones, on which he had to pay a duty of ten per cent. only. This privilege extended to his children and descendants in India, of which none can now be traced.

These Charters were issued in the fourth year of the reign of King James II. of England, and were signed by Benjamin Bathurst (Governor), Josiah Child (Deputy Governor), and three other officials. On the strength of the above charters or agreements, which were never questioned or annulled, the Armenians have at all times justly claimed their full rights to the enjoyment of equal privileges with the English in India.

From this it will be clearly seen that the Armenians, and Khojah Phanoos Khalanthar in particular, were held in high esteem by the Court of Directors for their strong attachment to the Company and their unswerving loyalty to the British cause in India.

The Hon'ble East India Company was readily anxious to cultivate the friendship of the Armenian merchants, who, being acquainted with all parts of the country and having a thorough knowledge of the vernacular, were of great help to them in pushing on the Company's trade in the interior. This fact is illustrated by an extract from a communication to the Indian Governor from the Court of Directors, dated 13th September 1695 :—

> "Multan and Scindy are brave provinces for many sorts of extraordinary good and cheap commodities; but whenever the Company shall be induced to settle factories in those provinces, or any other way think to arrive at trade with them, otherwise than by Armenians, they would infallibly come off with great loss." *

As fellow-traders, the Armenians rendered yeoman service to the Hon'ble East India Company, whose early records and proceedings teem with favourable references to them.

The probity of the Armenians in commercial matters had not escaped the attention of the English traders, and the latter were not slow to cultivate their friendship, which eventually stood them in good stead. In 1715, when an important deputation was sent by the Company to the Mogul Court at Delhi, the Armenians rendered a brilliant proof of their attachment to the English. The immediate necessity of a royal *firman* from the Mogul Emperor, granting them certain privileges, was keenly felt by the Company, who decided upon sending a mission

* This extract is also recopied from the *Calcutta Review*.

The communication (in which the original spelling has been preserved) goes on to say:—

"If you can procure any Armenian Christians to be souldiers, we doe allow you to give them the same pay as our English souldiers and forty shillings gratuity, and the charge of their passage from Gombroon * to Bombay. We would not have above fifty or sixty in our pay at one time; and if you had the like number of Madagascar slaves to teach the exercise of arms and to do some inferior duty under our English souldiers, being listed upon an English Captaine, kept in a company by themselves under the Dutch manner, and allowing them a competent proportion of rice, a red capp and red coat, and some other trifles to please them, not having above fifty or sixty at a time, and they never to have a custody of their own armes, we hope such a contrivance might be a good auxiliary aid to our garrison, especially when English souldiers are scarce, and [? we need] some ballance of power. For take it as an infallible constant rule, that the more castes the more safety and the less danger of mutiny. . . . We know there is a necessity for increasing our English souldiers, and we will do it as soone and as much as we possibly can. In the meantime, Armenian Christians, if you could have them, *are the very best men to be trusted;* and next to them, Madagascar Coffrees." †

---

* Gombroon is a commercial port in the Persian Gulf. It was afterwards called *Bunder Abbas, i.e.,* "the harbour of Abbas," in honour of Shah Abbas the Great, King of Persia, and which name it bears to the present day. The Armenian colonists of Julfa, Ispahan, reached this port *viâ* Yezd and Kerman by caravan, and from thence sailed to India. Traces of their sojourn at that port are to be seen at the present day in the shape of tombstones with Armenian inscriptions.

† This extract is recopied from the *Calcutta Review*, a quarterly periodical devoted to literature and history. It was established in 1844 by that eminent and enthusiastic scholar, the late Sir J. W. Kaye, before his return to England, where he died in 1876. He recorded of it:—"The best service which I ever rendered in India, or indeed *for* India, was the establishment, single-handed, of the *Calcutta Review*, which has done far more for Indian literature than anything I have written under my own name." This 'Record of Indian Thought,' as Sir Richard Temple designated it, after changing many hands during the past fifty years, is now owned, printed, and published by Mr. Thomas S. Smith at his City Press, 12 Bentinck Street, Calcutta.

From this it will be clearly seen that the Armenians, and Khojah Phanoos Khalanthar in particular, were held in high esteem by the Court of Directors for their strong attachment to the Company and their unswerving loyalty to the British cause in India.

The Hon'ble East India Company was readily anxious to cultivate the friendship of the Armenian merchants, who, being acquainted with all parts of the country and having a thorough knowledge of the vernacular, were of great help to them in pushing on the Company's trade in the interior. This fact is illustrated by an extract from a communication to the Indian Governor from the Court of Directors, dated 13th September 1695 :—

> "Multan and Scindy are brave provinces for many sorts of extraordinary good and cheap commodities; but whenever the Company shall be induced to settle factories in those provinces, or any other way think to arrive at trade with them, otherwise than by Armenians, they would infallibly come off with great loss." *

As fellow-traders, the Armenians rendered yeoman service to the Hon'ble East India Company, whose early records and proceedings teem with favourable references to them.

The probity of the Armenians in commercial matters had not escaped the attention of the English traders, and the latter were not slow to cultivate their friendship, which eventually stood them in good stead. In 1715, when an important deputation was sent by the Company to the Mogul Court at Delhi, the Armenians rendered a brilliant proof of their attachment to the English. The immediate necessity of a royal *firman* from the Mogul Emperor, granting them certain privileges, was keenly felt by the Company, who decided upon sending a mission

* This extract is also recopied from the *Calcutta Review*.

to the Mogul Court to represent their grievances and make certain favourable overtures. They saw the advisability of seeking the co-operation of an influential person, who would be instrumental in arranging for an interview, to accompany the mission to Delhi.

Khojah Israel Sarhad, an Armenian merchant of great eminence and vast influence, was selected, than whom an abler man could not have been found. Besides being "a considerable Armenian merchant," he had a thorough knowledge of English and Persian, the latter being the court language at Delhi. He responded in the characteristic Armenian spirit by accompanying Stephenson and Surman, the Company's factors, in their important mission to the Mogul Court, in the days of the Emperor Ferokhsiyar.

With reference to this important deputation, Bolts, in his *Considerations on Indian Affairs*, informs us:—

"The trade of the English Company in Bengal had, from the period of their submission to Aurungzebe, continued to grow daily more important, but it was not carried on without frequent interruptions from the officers of the Mogul government, which it was hardly possible to avoid with a colony so situated. Being sensible likewise of the precarious tenures of their establishments in Bengal and elsewhere, in the year 1715 the Company sent a deputation of two gentlemen to the court of Delhi: one an Englishman, named John Surman, and the other a very considerable Armenian merchant, named Cogee [Khojah] Serhaud, to solicit redress for past, and security against future, oppressions; for an extension of their old, and for many new, privileges; and particularly for a small spot of ground to be allowed them wherever they settled a factory."

Such was the humble language used by the English only forty years before the memorable battle of Plassey.

Its victory made the English the absolute masters of Bengal. The deputation reached Delhi on the 8th July of the same year (1715), but did not gain an interview immediately, as was customary in those days. The favourable moment arrived at last, and they were duly conducted into the Emperor's presence, to whom they presented the Company's petition with all due formalities. Khojah Sarhad, who was on terms of intimacy with the Emperor Ferokhsiyar, as will be seen hereafter, not merely acted as an eloquent spokesman, but as an able interpreter in making known to the Emperor the contents of the Company's petition, which prayed for many privileges, of which the following is a copy:—

"The cargoes of English ships, wrecked on the Mogul's coast, should be protected from plunder;

"that a fixed sum should be received at Surat in lieu of all duties;

"that three villages, contiguous to Madras, which had been granted, and again resumed, by the Government of Arcot, should be restored in perpetuity;

"that the port of Diu, near the port of Masulipatam, should be given to the Company for an annual rent;

"that all persons in Bengal who might be indebted to the Company, should be delivered up to the Presidency on the first demand;

"that a passport (*dustuck*), signed by the President of Calcutta, should exempt the goods which it specified from stoppage or examination by the officers of the Bengal Government; and

"that the Company should be permitted to purchase the zemindarship of thirty-seven towns in the same manner as they had been authorised by Azeem-us-Shaun to purchase Calcutta, Suttanaty, and Govindpore."

Khojah Sarhad explained and elucidated certain points in the petition, which his majesty did not seem to comprehend, and, chiefly through his exertions, the mission was brought to a successful conclusion. The following is also from Bolts:—

"It was upon this deputation that the English East India Company obtained their Grand *Firman*, exempting them from paying any duties upon their trade within the Mogul's dominions, on paying a *peshcush*, or acknowledgment, of ten thousand rupees per annum. As this is the *firman* by which they were governed till they themselves became the makers of nabobs and moguls, and will shew what parts of the petitions of our ambassadors were granted, we give it entire to our readers, in the translation which Mr. James Fraser, a gentleman well acquainted with the Persian language, has made of it, and inserted in his history of Nader Shah, *viz.*:—

"'ALL GOVERNORS, PEOPLE IN OFFICES, &c., who are at present, and shall be hereafter, in the province of Ahmedabad, and in the fortunate ports of Surat and Cambay, being in hopes of the royal favour, Know that at this time Mr. John Surman and Cogee [Khojah] Serhaud, factors to the English, have represented the customs on English goods all over the empire are pardoned, except at the port of Surat; and that at the said port from the time of the late Emperor, Shahab-al-Deen Shah Jehan, two per cent. was settled as customs; from the time of the late Emperor, Mohy-al-Deen Mahomed Aurungzebe Allumgheer, three and a half per cent. was appointed; and in other places none molested them on this account. And in the time of the Emperor, Abul Mazuffer Bahadr Shah, two and a half per cent. was settled, and is in force until now. By reason of the oppressions of the Government officers there, it is three years since they have withdrawn their factory. In the provinces of Behar and Orissa, this nation pays no customs; and in the port of Hoogly, in the province of Bengal, they yearly give 3,000 rupees' acknowledgment in lieu of customs; they are in hopes that, according to the custom of other ports, in the port of Surat likewise a yearly acknowledgment may be settled in lieu of customs. They agree therefore to a yearly *peshcush*, or acknowledgment, of ten thousand rupees.

"'The order that subjects the world to obey it, and which must be strictly followed, is issued forth: that since they agree to ten thousand rupees' *peshcush* at the port of Surat, take it yearly; and, besides that, molest them on no account. And what goods or effects their factors bring or carry away, by land or water, to and from the ports of the provinces and other parts, looking upon them to be custom free, let them buy and sell at their pleasure. And if in any place, any of their effects should be stolen, use your utmost endeavours to recover them, delivering the robbers to punishment and the goods to the owner; and wherever they settle a factory, or buy and sell goods, be assisting to them on all just occasions, and whomsoever of the merchants, etc., they may have a just demand on by accounts, according to equity, give the English their due, and let no person injure their factors. They have likewise humbly represented "That the Dewans in the provinces may demand the original *sunnud*, or a copy, with the Nazim or Dewan's seal affixed, that to produce the original in every place is impracticable; they are therefore in hopes that a copy under the Kazy's seal shall be credited, and they not demand the original Sunnud, or molest them on account of a copy, with the Nazim or Dewan's seal. And, in the island of Bombay, belonging to the English, where Portuguese coins are current, that, according to the custom of Madrass coins may be struck: and that whoever of the Company's servants, being in debt, runs away, may be sent to the chief of the factory; and that on account of the Fowzdary,* and other forbidden articles (by which means the Company's factors and servants are vexed and discouraged), they be not molested."

"'The strict and high order is issued forth, that a copy, under the Kazy's seal, be credited; and that in the island of Bombay fortunate coins, struck according to the custom of the empire, be current; and whosoever of the Company's servants, being indebted, runs away, let him be taken and delivered to the chief of the factory, and let them not be molested on account of the forbidden articles. They have likewise represented "That in Bengal, Behar, and Orissa the Company have factories, and they are willing to settle in other places. They are in hopes, that wherever they settle *forty begas*† *of ground* may be graciously bestowed on them by the Emperor; and that their ships sometimes, by reason of tempests, run ashore and are wrecked, and that the Governors of the ports do, in an oppressive manner, seize the goods, and in some places demand a quarter part," the royal order is issued forth, that they act according to the customs of the factories in other provinces in regard to this nation, who have factories in the Imperial ports and dealings at court, and have miraculously obtained a Firmaun, exempting them from customs. Take care, in a just manner, of the goods of their ships that are wrecked or have lost their passage; and in all affairs act according to this great order, and demand not a

* The *fousdar* in all great cities is the magistrate for licensing of disorderly houses and the sales of spirituous liquors, and takes cognizance of riots, &c.: on which account, by the irregularities of the English sailors, the Company's servants were frequently exposed to difficulties. This relieved them from the *fousdar's* jurisdiction.—*Bolts.*

† Say, 15 acres; a *bega*, or *bigha*, being about 16,003 square feet.

new grant yearly. In this be punctual. Written on the 4th of Saffer in the Fifth year of this glorious reign'" (the 6th January 1716-17).

Indian historians have invariably attributed the success of this mission to the scientific skill of William Hamilton, a surgeon in the service of the Hon'ble East India Company. He died at Calcutta on 4th December 1717, where his tombstone, with inscriptions in English and Persian, can be seen at the Charnock Mausoleum in St. John's churchyard. He had been appointed as surgeon to the embassy, which was composed of Messrs. John Surman and Edward Stephenson of the Company's service, and Khojah Israel Sarhad, already referred to.

Dr. Harvey, who presided at the Indian Medical Congress held at Calcutta in December 1894, expatiated at great length, in his opening address, on the valuable services rendered to the Hon'ble East India Company by their doctors in the olden times. He made special mention of Dr. Gabriel Boughton of Surat, and Surgeon William Hamilton of Calcutta, who have found a niche in the history of India, and "to whose skill in their profession, and loyal patriotism," he said "the earliest successes of the British in India owed so much."

With due deference to the learned speaker, and in no way disparaging the skill of Surgeon William Hamilton, I venture to assert that the success of this important embassy should be mainly attributed not to him, but to the strenuous exertions of the Armenian, Khojah Israel Sarhad, without whose powerful influence at court the timely services of Surgeon Hamilton would not have been called into requisition by the ailing Emperor, with whom Khojah Sarhad was on intimate terms.

Through the courtesy of Professor C. R. Wilson (referred to particularly in the Preface), who placed at my disposal copies of parts of the Company's Proceedings obtained from the India Office authorities, I am in a position to support my statements regarding the history of the mission, by placing before my readers certain important facts, in connection with the embassy, in which Khojah Sarhad played so prominent a part. These valuable extracts are culled from the early Proceedings and Records of the Hon'ble East India Company, the originals of which are kept in the archives of the India Office in London. They are as follow:—

"28th January 1713.

"One of the Calcutta merchants, Cojah Sarhaud (an Armenian) had owed the Company money for some time, and he had no effects in Calcutta wherewith to pay it, but he told the Company that he had goods enough, and more than enough, to pay the debt with in Goa. He had also a vessel of his own at Calcutta laden with merchandise bought of the Company, but not paid for. The Councill agreed to let the money for their own goods stand over and to send Cojah Sarhaud's vessel under Captain Delafosse to Goa to fetch the merchandise he had there. Cojah Sarhaud therefore made over his property in Goa to the amount that he was indebted to the Company to the United Councill as follows:—

"'*Whereas* I, Cojah Sarhaud Armenian of Calcutta in Bengall merchant, am this day indebted to the Hon'ble United Company of merchants of England, trading to the East Indies the full sum of Thirty-eight thousand eight hundred and thirty-one rupees two annas: *And whereas* in the year 1710 I sent effects for my own account to Goa to the amount of about Seventy-five thousand rupees, consigned to my factor Avenoose [Johanness], who being dead the effects are now in the hands of Aga Peerie who succeeded him as my factor in Goa, and for which I have as yet received no returns: *Be it known unto all men* by these presents that I Cojah Sarhaud do hereby make over and assign all my right title and interest in the said effects and their produce at Goa unto the Hon'ble the President and Councill in Bengall for security of the debt principals and interest due from me to the said Hon'ble United Company of merchants of England, trading ' the East Indies. *In witness whereof* I have hereunto set, my hand and seal in Fort Wiillam in Bengall the 27th January 17$\frac{32}{8}$.'"*

———:o:———

"After receiving this document, the Councill wrote the following letters (1) to Captain Delafosse and (2) to the Viceroy of Goa:—

"'Captain Delafosse

"'Your vessel the *Blenheim* having on board her all the goods designed to be laden on her by Cojah Sarhaud which he has consigned to yourself, you are hereby ordered immediately to weigh anchor and proceed with all possible expedition to Goa and there dispose of your cargoe the best you can. Senr. Augustine Robero and Cojah Narur are Cojah Sarhaud's attorneys in Goa, and you are to receive from them or the person that shall be present of them the produce of such goods and effects as they receive from Aga Perie belonging to Cojah Sarhaud; and if all you shall receive from them does not amount to considerably a greater sum than the Thirty-thousand rupees you are to receive it aboard your sloop and return with it to us with all possible expedition, out of the produce whereof we will take care that your wages and the wages of your sloop's company shall be paid. But if what shall be delivered you amounts to a much greater sum than Thirty-thousand rupees as Cojah Sarhaud assures us it will, you are in that case if a good ship may be bought reasonably cheap at Goa to assist Cojah Sarhaud's attorneys or the person that shall be present of them with your advice in buying her; and we order when she is bought that you quit the sloop and take the command of the ship on you and that Walter Welsh be your mate aboard her, and that you receive aboard her all Cojah Sarhaud's effects that shall be delivered you leaving nothing to be put aboard the sloops till you have the amount of at least Fifty-thousand rupees aboard the ships, and when you have that full amount aboard her we consent if Cojah Sarhaud's attorney or attorneys desire it that what shall remain be laden aboard the sloop. And we enjoin you to take what care you can to see that the person appointed to be master of her be a seaman fitly qualified to take charge of her, he must receive his orders from you and you are to order him to make the best of his way directly for Calcutta in Bengall.

"'If no ships proper for that service can for a reasonable price be bought at Goa and if there be a ship there belonging to Englishmen and bound for Bengall, we consent that so much of Cojah Sarhaud's effects as shall exceed the amount of Thirty-thousand rupees to be laden on freight on board her, but we would have the full amount of Thirty-thousand rupees be with you aboard the sloop.

"'If it should happen (which God forbid) that you shall get nothing from Cojah Sarhaud's factor or attorneys in Goa of the

* The original spelling and punctuation have been followed.

effects he says he has there bring the returns in Arrack or anything else you can get that is proper for this market for the produce of the small cargoe now aboard you and stay no longer at Goa than the last day of August if no misfortune or unforeseen accident do not detain you. . . .

"'In case you have the misfortune not to save your passage to Goa (which God forbid) follow such directions as Cojah Sarhaud shall give you about disposing of your cargoe at any port where you shall be obliged to stay and proceed thence by such conveyance as you shall judge best either by sea or land to Goa with the letters and other papers mentioned in those instructions. We wish you a prosperous voyage and are

"'Your loving friends

(This document was signed by all the Councill)

"Fort William, 28th January $17\frac{12}{8}$.'"

—:O:—

"'To His Excellency the Viceroy of Goa and General of all His Majestie the King of Portugall's Forces in the East Indies.

"'May it please your Excellency

"'The fame of your great wisdom and justice is heard everywhere and 'tis with delight we are entertained by persons of the best note coming from Goa with discourses in your praise. From them we find encouragement to address Your Excellency in favour of Cojah Sarhaud an Armenian merchant inhabiting this place under our protection and government; his affairs will be made known to Your Excellency in few words by his attorneys in Goa and he will submit entirely to the sentence Your Excellency shall judge to be the merit of his cause. We are with profound respect

"'Your Excellency's most humble Servants

"'Robert Hedges
Abram Addams
Samll Feake
James Williamson
Edw. Page
Samll Browne
John Deane'"

—:O:—

"The Councill also sentt letters to the two following men on the same subject and of the same substance as the letter to the Viceroy (*i.e.*) to Robert Adams Esq. Chief for the affairs of the Hon'ble United Company of Merchants of England trading to the East Indies in Calicutt, and to the Chief and Councill for the affairs of the Hon'ble United Company of Merchants of England trading to the East Indies and Carwar.

"27th January 1713-1714.

"Reasons for appointing Cojah Sarhaud second in the negotiations at the Great Mogul's Court:*

"'1st He managed our affairs in Mahomed Azeem's Durbar and by his prudent conduct and winning address insinuated himself into favour and procured for us the Grant of this place and the dependant Towns which we now enjoy, and that for a small expence in comparison of the benefit.

"'2nd He was personally known to Prince Feruckseer the present King then about fourteen years old and made him presents of toys at that time very acceptable, for which he exprest a great deal of satisfaction often sending for Cojah Surhaud and making him sit by him many hours to show what uses they were for. This we believe the King remembers and is probably one cause of his readily ordering a *Husbull Hookum* for us at the request of Cojah Surhaud's friends and agents at Court, and appointing him to be particularly named in that, and all the *Perwannas* we lately received, commanding safe conduct for him also for our Present and English Gentlemen that shall accompany it.

"'3rd It is absolutely necessary that some person who is perfect master of the Persian language and understands our affairs very well and what may be useful for us be sent and we know no man so qualified in both these respects as Cojah Surhaud is. He is therefore the fittest man we can send.

"'4th If we should send him as Vacqueel only and inferior to all the English Gentlemen we may reasonably suppose the King would in that case regard him most, which would be an affront to our nation. But that is not now likely to happen because he is joined in commission, and second in negotiation and it will be his interest to get favour and respect for the whole.

"'5th The English Gentlemen are sent because they may be a check on him on all occasions and see that he does not misapply the Company's goods or money nor be more expensive on any occasion than is absolutely necessary.

"All which considerations being unanimously agreed to, we do appoint that Mr John Surman be first, Cojah Sur-

* The five reasons adduced thinly disguise the fact that Khojah Sarhad was practically *first* in negotiations, and that he could, of his own influence, have secured the advantages which the Council sought. To be obliged to seek privileges through this Armenian was evidently distasteful to the Council; and they would have sent him "as Vacqueel," or in an inferior position, if they had dared to risk success. Reason No. 5 might be regarded as a slur upon Khojah Sarhad's character—it was, however, a prudent safeguard, and it afforded a pretext for "the English Gentlemen" accompanying him,—but Reason No. 1, which depicts his probity in a similar matter, shuts out any suggestion against his character.

haud second, and Mr John Pratt, third in this negotiation and that they consult together upon all occasions and act according to the result of their consultations. And that they may not want sufficient help nor have any reasonable cause to keep the accounts of their Transactions or of expences behind hand we do appoint Mr Edwd Stephenson, Secretary and accomptant to the negotiation and we order that he be present, and [take down] the minutes when they sit in consultation.

"Cojah Surhaud being thus elected second in this negotiation, the Terms* agreed to with him are next to be explained, and those are—

"'*First.* If all the privileges the Company have at any time heretofore enjoyed in the Mogull's dominions be confirmed in the new *Phirmaund* and if he gets our bounds enlarged as far as we desire southward to near Kidderpoor and that the shore on the side of the river opposite to this place be also granted us. Also if he endeavour earnestly to get the grant of the Dew [Diu] Island near Metchlepatam [Masulipatam], which the President and Councill at Madras desire may be obtained for that Presidency. His reward is then to be Fifty-thousand Rupees but he is to have nothing if he fails in those points.

"'*Secondly.* If he procures the privilege of our nation to trade custom free at Suratt which he will attempt, he is to have Fifty-thousand Rupees more for that service, but if he fails in that he is not to have the reward. He is nevertheless to endeavour to get the custom we pay at that port reduced to 2½ per cent.'

"It was also unanimously agreed that Cojah Surhaud whose interest, etc. at Court has already had the good effect of procuring us the *Hasbull Hukum* and several other useful orders from Court be sent to assist in suing for the kings *Phirmand* and that he sit and vote in Councill along with the three English Gentlemen."

———:o:———

"19th October 1713.

"Cojah Surhaud wrote last July to Cojah Manoor who formerly was chief eunuch to Mahumed Azeem the father of King Furruckseer and is now entitled Nazur

* The terms are couched very craftily. If Khojah Sarhad had been equally crafty in his dealings with the English, he might have disavowed their cause at the critical moment, and have obtained a *firman* for his own nation.

Cawne [Khan] his present office is to attend Patshaw Begum the daughter of Aurungzeeb. This Razir Cawne's intercession prevailed with the King to order a *Hasbull Hookum* to be given ordering all Subahs, Governors and Officers whatsoever to guard our present for the King through their several Governments till it shall arrive with the English that shall accompany it and Cojah Surhaud at Court. This *Hasbull Hookum* being arrived under a cover to Coja Surhaud at Delly, write him the King has ordered another *Hasbull Hookum* for us to pass all the English trade in his dominions, with the usual freedom till the Royall *Phirmaund* is obtained. Cojah Surhaud flatters us with hopes that the second *Hasbull Hookum* may be with us in a few days."

———:o:———

"22nd October.

"This day, Cojah Surhaud laid before us the *Hasbull Hookum* which came yesterday to his hand (*i.e.*) to Mursond Cooly Cawne now Jaffer Cawne Neib Subah of Bengall

"Keyrat Cawne Subah [of] Patna

"Cawne Jean Behader now Acyudula Subah of Illabad [Allahabad]

"Rajah Chevilram Subah of Ectstarabad:

"all relating to the safe conveyance of our present and English Ambassadors to the Mogulls Court. These are sealed up with the seal of Tuckurrum Cawne the King's Jeweller and great master of his wardrobe. But copies are brought open to us and we find they are confirmations of the *Hasbull Hookums* which Cojah Surhaud delivered open to us on the 19th current."

CHAPTER VI.

BRITISH SUPREMACY IN THE ASCENDANT.

THE object of the important mission to Delhi—to obtain the GRAND FIRMAN—was secured for the English mainly through the diplomatic talents of Khojah Sarhad, who in 1698 had also been instrumental in procuring from Prince Mahomed Azim-us-Shaun "the Grant of this place [Calcutta] and its dependant Towns, and that for a small expense in comparison of the benefit."

Stewart, in his *History of Bengal*, states that "the inhabitants of Calcutta enjoyed, after the return of the Embassy, a degree of freedom and security unknown to the other subjects of the Mogul Empire, and that city increased yearly in wealth, beauty and riches."

For several years after this mission, the English in Bengal were engaged in the peaceful and lucrative pursuits of commerce, in friendly rivalry with the Armenians, "whose commerce," says Bolts, "was likewise established by the Mogul's *firman*," &c.

Nothing eventful occurred until the memorable year 1756. Ali Verdi Khan, the last of the great nawabs of Bengal and the Viceroy of the Mogul Emperor of Delhi, died in that year. He was succeeded by his grandson, Suraj-ud-Dowlah, a youth of only eighteen summers, but nevertheless a monster-incarnate of cruelty and lust. Throughout his boyhood he had been an inveterate enemy of the English with whom he had a rupture only a few months after his succession.

The English, having heard of the near prospect of a war with the French in Europe, had, without obtaining the Nawab's permission, secured their fortifications at Calcutta against the French, who, according to Marshman, "had more than ten times the number of European soldiers at Chandernagore than the English had at Calcutta." They had also afforded shelter to one Kristna Das, a rich native, and a subject of the Nawab, who, on the 17th of March (1756), had fled to Calcutta to escape the rapacity of Suraj-ud-Dowlah. These were the grounds on which he declared war against the English, and, at the head of an army of 50,000 men, marched from Murshidabad to Calcutta, attacked and captured the old fort* of the English, which included the Company's factory. Then was enacted the tragedy of the Black Hole† of Calcutta. Macaulay, in his critical essay on Lord Clive, thus graphically describes its unparalleled horrors:—

* The *old fort*, with its adjoining warehouses, covered the site of the present General Post Office, the Collectorate, Custom House, Fairlie Place, and Coila Ghat Street It was erected in 1698, and was named 'Fort William' after William III. In 1819, a portion was pulled down to make room for the Custom House, and the remainder was removed in 1856, when the General Post Office was built.

† The historical *Black Hole* of Calcutta, a dungeon 18 feet square with only two small barred windows, was the military jail of *old* Fort William. Its site was commemorated by an obelisk fifty feet high. This monument, erected at the expense of Mr. Holwell, one of the survivors was once struck by lightning in 1819. It was pulled down by order of the Governor-General of that time, the Earl of Moira and Marquis of Hastings (who should not be confounded with Warren Hastings), on the ground that "it served to remind the natives of the country of the former humiliation of the English." With greater reason it might be said to have reminded the natives of the determination and prowess of the British, who, stimulated by the cowardly *Black Hole* tragedy, had avenged its atrocities and asserted their power and supremacy over Bengal at the battle of Plassey. A simple tablet, on the inner side of the gate dividing the General Post Office and the Calcutta Collectorate, indicates the site (its size being illustrated by flagstones) of the Black Hole.

"Then was committed that great crime, memorable for its singular atrocity, memorable for the tremendous retribution by which it was followed. The English captives were left to the mercy of the guards, and the guards determined to secure them for the night in the prison of the garrison, a chamber known by the fearful name of the Black Hole. Even for a single European malefactor that dungeon would, in such a climate, have been too close and narrow. The space was only twenty feet square; the air-holes were small and obstructed. It was the summer solstice, the season when the fierce heat of Bengal can scarcely be rendered tolerable to natives of England by lofty halls and by the constant waving of fans. The number of the prisoners was one hundred and forty-six. When they were ordered to enter the cell, they imagined that the soldiers were joking; and, being in high spirits, on account of the promise of the Nabob to spare their lives, they laughed and jested at the absurdity of the notion. They soon discovered their mistake. They expostulated; they entreated: but in vain. The guards threatened to cut down all who hesitated. The captives were driven into the cell at the point of the sword, and the door was instantly shut and locked upon them.

"Nothing in history or fiction, not even the story which Ugolino told in the sea of everlasting ice, after he had wiped his bloody lips on the scalp of his murderer, approaches the horrors which were recounted by the few survivors of that night. They cried for mercy. They strove to burst the door. Holwell, who, even in that extremity, retained some presence of mind, offered large bribes to the gaolers. But the answer was that nothing could be done without the Nabob's orders, that the Nabob was asleep, and that he would be angry if anybody woke him. Then the prisoners went mad with despair. They trampled each other down, fought for the places at the windows, fought for the pittance of water with which the cruel mercy of the murderers mocked their agonies, raved, prayed, blasphemed, implored the guards to fire among them! The gaolers in the meantime held lights to the bars, and shouted with laughter at the frantic struggles of their victims! At length the tumult died away in low gaspings and moanings. The day broke. The Nabob had slept off his debauch, and permitted the door to be opened. But it was some time before the soldiers could make a lane for the survivors, by piling up on each side the heaps of corpses on which the burning climate had already begun to do its loathsome work. When at length a passage was made, twenty-three ghastly figures, such as their own mothers would not have known, staggered one by one out of the charnel-house. A pit was instantly dug. The dead bodies, a hundred and twenty-three in number, were flung into it promiscuously, and covered up.

"But these things, which, after the lapse of more than eighty years, cannot be told or read without horror, awakened neither remorse nor pity in the bosom of the savage Nabob. He inflicted no punishment on the murderers. He showed no tenderness to the survivors. Some of them, indeed, from whom nothing was to be got, were suffered to depart; but those from whom it was thought that anything could be extorted were treated with execrable cruelty. Holwell, unable to walk, was carried before the tyrant, who reproached him, threatened him, and sent him up the country in irons, together with some other gentlemen who were suspected of knowing more than they chose to tell about the treasures of the Company. These persons, still bowed down by the sufferings of that great agony, were lodged in miserable sheds, and fed only with grain and water, till at length the intercessions of the female relations of the Nabob procured their release. One English woman* had survived that night. She was placed in the harem of the Prince at Moorshedabad."

* She was the heroic Mrs. Carey, "a fine country-born lady," as Holwell calls her, who accompanied her husband, one of the officers of the ship, to the Black Hole, when all the ladies had left the Fort and taken refuge in the ships.

Some who took refuge in ships, among whom was Drake, the Governor of Calcutta, dropped down with the tide and anchored off Fulta, on the left bank of the river Hoogly, about forty miles distant from Calcutta. They were suffering privations for want of provisions, when Khojah* Petrus Arratoon, a well-known Armenian merchant of Calcutta, and a man of vast influence, secretly supplied them for about six months—during the interval between the tragedy of the Black Hole and the arrival of the Army of Retribution from Madras—with *boat-loads* of provisions from Calcutta.

Occasionally he visited his friends, the English, at Fulta, where he was always warmly welcomed by them. He was there, on that memorable day, the 20th December 1756, when the avenging army, under Clive and Admiral Watson, arrived from Madras. Calcutta was recovered after little fighting, and the Nawab sued for peace. Khojah Petrus was afterwards employed by Clive as a confidential agent in negotiating with Meer Jaffier for the overthrow of Nawab Suraj-ud-Dowlah.

The following extracts in connection with these negotiations are taken from the second volume of Orme's *History of Hindoostan*:—

"The day after the conference between Omichand and Latty, *Petrus the Armenian*, who had been employed between the Nabob and the English in February, came to Mr. Watts† [in April] with the same proposals from Meer Jaffier as had been made by Latty" (p. 148).

"He [Mr. Watts] at the same time despatched Mr. Scrofton as the Select Committee, and on the 6th

---

* *Khojah* is a corrupted form of the Persian word خواجه *Khwajeh*, signifying a man of distinction, a gentleman, a rich merchant.

† Mr. Watts was at that time the British Resident at Murshidabad, where the Nawabs of Bengal had their seat of government.

May [1757] received their resolutions concerning the treaty with Jaffier, who in concert with Jaffier's Agent, who we suppose to be still *the Armenian Petrus*, they established positive sums to the articles stipulating monies" (p. 156).

"He [Mr. Watts] however immediately [June 1757] sent away *the Armenian Petrus* who had been the most confidential of his Agents in the conspiracy, and Jaffier sent one of his domestics with Petrus. Both were instructed to press Colonel Clive to begin his march" (p. 165).

"The *Armenian Petrus* with the messenger from Meer Jaffier arrived the same day" (p. 167).

At the close of the battle of Plassey on 23rd June 1757, Meer Jaffier joined his forces with the English, and on 29th June Clive placed him on the viceregal throne at Murshidabad.

The following is a copy of the Treaty (the original of which was in Persian) between Clive on behalf of the East India Company and Meer Jaffier Ally Khawn upon being invested with the Nabobship of Bengal:—

"I swear by God and the Prophet of God, to abide by the terms of this Treaty whilst I have life.*

(Sd.) "MEER MAHOMED JAFFIER KHAWN BAHADER,
"*Servant to* KING ALLUM GUEER.

"1. Whatever articles were agreed upon in the time of peace with the Nabob Serajah-al-Dowlah, Munsur-al-Muluk, Shah Kuly Khawn Bahader Hybut Jung. I agree to comply with.

"2. The enemies of the English are my enemies, whether they be Indians or Europeans.

"3. All the effects and factories belonging to the French in the province of Bengal (the Paradise of Nations) and Bahar, and Orissa, shall remain in the possession of the English, nor will I ever allow them any more to settle in the Three Provinces

"4. In consideration of the losses which the English Company have sustained by the capture and plunder of Calcutta by the Nabob,

---

* These lines, according to Bolts, were written and attested by Nawab Meer Jaffier's own hand.

and the charges occasioned by the maintenance of the forces, I will give them one crore of rupees.

"5. For the effects plundered from the English inhabitants at Calcutta, I agree to give fifty lacs of rupees.

"6. For the effects plundered from the Gentoos, Mussulmen, and other subjects of Calcutta, twenty lacs of rupees shall be given.

"7. For the effects plundered from the Armenian inhabitants of Calcutta, I will give the sum of seven lacs of rupees. The distribution of the sums allotted the natives, the English inhabitants, Gentoos, and Mussulmen, shall be left to the Admiral and Colonel Clive (Sabut Jung Bahader) and the rest of the Council, to be disposed of by them to whom they think proper.

"8. Within the ditch which surrounds the borders of Calcutta are tracts of land belonging to several zemindars; besides this. I will grant the English Company six hundred yards without the ditch.

"9. All the land lying south of Calcutta, as far as Culpee, shall be under the zemindary of the English Company and all the Officers of those parts shall be under their jurisdiction. The revenues to be paid by them (the Company) in the same manner with other zemindars.

"10. Whenever I demand the English assistance, I will be at the charge of the maintenance of them.

"11. I will not erect any new fortifications below Hoogly, near the river Ganges.

"12. As soon as I am established in the Government of the Three Provinces, the aforesaid sums shall be faithfully paid. Dated 15th Ramzan, in the 4th year of the reign."

Additional Article.

"13 On condition that Meer Jaffier Khawn Bahader shall solemnly ratify, confirm by oath, and execute all the above articles, which the under-written on behalf of the Honourable East India Company do, declaring on the Holy Gospels, and before God, that we will assist Meer Jaffier Khawn Bahader with all our force, to obtain the subahship of the Provinces of Bengal, Bahar, and Orissa; and further that we will assist him to the utmost against all his enemies whatever, as soon as he calls upon us for that end; provided that he, on his coming to be Nabob, shall fulfil the aforesaid articles."

Khojah Petrus Arratoon* was held in high esteem for his piety and charitable disposition, and was regarded

* *Khojah* was a titular distinction (see footnote to p. 69); *Petrus* was his baptismal name; and *Arratoon* his father's name. Prior to the nineteenth century it was customary for Armenians to adopt their father's name as a surname. although they were familiarly known by their own Christian baptismal name; hence he was known as Khojah Petrus. Ancestral names, as far as they can be traced, are now adopted by Armenians.

as the leader of the Armenian community of Calcutta. He died at the age of fifty-three on the 29th August 1778. His revered tomb, bearing a long inscription in metrical Armenian verse, may be seen in the choir of the Armenian Church of St. Nazareth, Calcutta, where he was buried. His widow, who died in 1805, lies beside him.

A notable instance of their pristine warlike spirit was revived in Khojah Gregory. He was the son of Khalanthar Arratoon of Julfa and a brother of the famous Khojah Petrus already referred to. Khojah Gregory is better known, however, in Indian history by his orientalised name, Gorgin Khan.* An Armenian contemporary writer says that he was a merchant by profession, and had resided at the Court of Murshidabad for many years with numbers of his countrymen, who were afterwards connected with him in the army, which he raised and disciplined for the Nawab Meer Kasim, with whom he had formed a most intimate friendship.

Meer Jaffier Ali, who had succeeded Suraj-ud-Dowlah as Nawab of Bengal, was deposed by the English in 1760 on the grounds of being incapable to rule; and his son-in-law, Meer Kasim, was created by the English as Subadar of Bengal, in consideration of his ceding to them the three important districts of Burdwan, Midnapore, and Chittagong. Meer Kasim then appointed Gorgin Khan as his Chief Minister and Commander of all his Forces. Through personal ability he rose to eminence in the service of the Nawab, who had entrusted into his able hands the reins of his vast army. Holwell writes of him:—

* *Gorgin* is the Persian for *Gregory*. Formerly *Khan* was a military title, *Khojah* being a civic distinction.

"Khojah Gregory is in the highest degree of favour with the Nawab [Meer Kasim] and his adherents, and has posts of the greatest trust near the Nawab's person; and through him the Armenians in general are setting up an independent footing in this country, and carrying on a trade greatly detrimental to our investments in all parts,"* &c.

Marshman, too, who is regarded as the best authority on Indian history of that time, has the following:—

"Meer Cassim met the difficulties of his position with great energy. He curtailed the extravagance of the Court establishments. He abolished the 'Ram Office,' the 'Antelope Office,' the 'Nightingale Office,' and many other useless and costly appendages of the menagerie department. He subjected the public accounts to a severe scrutiny, and obliged the officers to disgorge the plunder they had acquired. He exacted all arrears of rent with unexampled rigour, revised the assessment of the land, and made an addition of a crore of rupees to the annual revenue of the three provinces. These measures gave him the means of discharging all the obligations he had contracted to the English, after which he gave his entire attention to the great object of emancipating himself from the pressure of their authority, and restoring freedom to the Soobah. He removed the seat of Government to Monghir,† a distance of 320 miles from Calcutta, where, free from observations, he prosecuted his plans of independence with such earnestness that, in less than three years, he considered himself in a position to set their power at defiance. For this rapid progress he was mainly indebted to the exertions of an *Armenian*, born at Ispahan, generally known by his orientalized name of Gurghin Khan. He was originally a cloth-seller at Hooghly, but when entrusted with the

* This extract is recopied from the *Calcutta Review*.

† Marshman, in his *History of Bengal*, says:—"The fame which this town still enjoys for skill in the manufacture of muskets owes its origin to this Gurghin Khan, whose age at this time did not exceed thirty years."

responsibilities of office, turned out to be a man of original genius and vast resources. In less than three years he created a force of 15,000 cavalry and 25,000 infantry, disciplined on the modes of the Company's army; he manufactured firelocks, which were superior to the Tower-proof muskets; he established a foundry for casting cannon, and trained up a corps of artillerymen who would have done credit to the Company's service Nothing was wanting to render Meer Cassim more powerful than Ali Verdy Khan had ever been, but a few years of undisturbed leisure."

Leaving out of sight the fact that Gorgin Khan's energies were directed against the English, is there an Armenian whose heart will not thrill with joy on reading such an eulogistic account of one of his countrymen, from the pen of so learned an author? Every Armenian should feel proud that Gorgin Khan, the once humble "cloth-seller at Hooghly," as Marshman describes him, and comparatively an uneducated man, should have succeeded, by personal merit and the simple force of his native genius, in raising and organising a large and well-disciplined army; in establishing a foundry at Monghyr for casting cannon; in manufacturing firelocks considered superior to those made in England in those days; and in placing the administration of a large province on a firm, sound basis;—and all those, too, within the short space of three years.

"The unprincipled conduct of the Council Board in Calcutta," as Marshman styles it, and which eventually deprived Meer Kasim of his throne, brought on a rupture between him and the English, which resulted in several battles that were fought between the two armies. The last of these well-contested battles was fought at a place called Gheriah, on that memorable day the 2nd of August 1763, regarding which Marshman writes :—

"The battle lasted four hours, and, in the opinion of Clive, never did troops fight better than those of the Nabob. At one period of the action, indeed, they penetrated the English lines and captured two guns, and victory appeared for a time likely to incline to them, but the gallantry of the Europeans and the steadiness of the sepoys bore down all opposition, and the Nabob's troops were constrained to abandon all their guns and stores, and retreat to Oodwanulla."

A week after the battle of Gheriah, Gorgin Khan met his death at the hands of one or more assassins, who are said to have been instigated by the Nawab Meer Kasim. Marshman, in his *History of Bengal*, gives the following version of it :—

"It came out that in the evening three or four Moguls had entered his tent, and slain him. It was given out that they had gone to the Commander to ask for their arrears of pay, but he had ordered them to be driven away, on which they drew their swords and murdered him. The fact was, that no pay was then due to them; they had been paid nine days previously. At all events, this seems in a manner certain that Kasim Ali had treacherously sent them to kill his Commander-in-Chief, Gurghin Khan. A brother of the latter, named Khojah Petroos [the Armenian Petrus], resided in Calcutta, and was on terms of great friendship with Messrs. Vansittart and Hastings. He had secretly written a letter to Gurghin, urging him to quit the Nawab's service, and if he had a good opportunity to make him a prisoner. The Nawab's chief spy got intimation of this, and went at one o'clock at night to his master, and put him on his guard, by informing him that his Commander-in-Chief was a traitor. Within twenty-four hours of that time the Armenian General, Gurghin Khan, one of the greatest men of the age, was a corpse."

There is no evidence that Gorgin Khan had ever intrigued with his brother; on the contrary, his extraordinary talents in military matters had been wholly devoted to Nawab Meer Kasim's cause, and not even the fraternal affection that he had for his brother Petrus, who was in such high favour with the opposing forces, could have seduced him from his unswerving loyalty to the Nawab. The Armenian contemporary writer already referred to says that, when the English secretly wrote and asked him to make a prisoner of the Nawab, for which he would be handsomely rewarded, he replied:—

"I was a humble individual, Kasim Ali Khan trusted and raised me to this high post of honour, so I cannot [comply with your request]. Far from it that I should betray my master, particularly as it is a distinct national characteristic of the Armenians never to betray their masters, but serve them faithfully and remain always loyal to them."

He was a pious Christian, and sent for an Armenian priest, to whom he humbly confessed his sins and received the Blessed Sacrament at his hands with great faith and devotion before he expired. His body was removed from the camp with great solemnity and honour, and was buried in the village of Brae, where Sumru had encamped with his regiment.

A man remarkable for his genius and foresight, Gorgin Khan played a prominent part in the history of those times, and would probably have distinguished himself more in the early days of the British conquest of Bengal, had he not fallen a prey to the sword of an assassin, which sad event prematurely closed his illustrious career on Monday, the 11th August 1763.

Gorgin Khan had gathered round him about one hundred brave Armenians from various places, some of whom he appointed as officers over the army of which he had the full command. The following is a list of the nine colonels or commandants who served under him; these, with the exception of Sumru, were Armenians whom he constantly kept with their respective regiments in readiness for military service :—

(1) The first was that notorious adventurer Sumru.*

(2) Margar Johanness, Khalanthar, from Julfa.

(3) Arratoon Margar, a native of Julfa.

(4) Gregory Nahapiet Ayvazean, a native of Julfa.

---

* He was born of obscure parents at Treves, on the Moselle in the duchy of Luxemburg, Germany, and was either a Swiss or a German by birth. He found his way out to India as a sailor in the French navy. Shortly after his arrival in India, he deserted and joined the British in Bengal, where he bore the name of Walter Summers, of which Sumru or Sombre was the corrupted form. His real name, however, was Walter Reinhardt He in turn deserted the English and took service again under the French at Chandernagore as a serjeant. He next deserted the French a second time, and entered the service of Meer Kasim, the Nawab of Bengal. After the tragic death of Gorgin Khan, the Commander-in-Chief, who had refused to comply with the Nawab's desire to put to death the English that were at the Factory in Patna, the hideous task was undertaken by this inhumane, unprincipled desperado. About 200 of the Nawab's prisoners at Patna, amongst whom were three Members of Council, *viz.*, Ellis, Hay, and Lushington, fell by his hand on the night of the 5th October 1763. The English Government had offered a reward of Rs. 40,000 for his capture, but he made good his escape. After serving different native chiefs, he finally entered the service of Mirza Najif Khan Minister of the Emperor Shah Alum II., from whom he received the village of Sirdhana, near Meerut, as a *jagir*. He died in 1778 at Agra, and, with shame be it said, lies buried in a handsome mausoleum at the old Christian cemetery of that place, called 'Padre Santo' by the natives, where, according to Keene, in his interesting *Handbook to Agra*, "the older inscriptions are all in the Armenian character." Sumru was succeeded in his *jagir* by his supposed widow, the notorious Begum Sumru, originally a Muhammadan dancing girl and a native of Cashmere. According to Bishop Heber, she was, in 1823, a "a little queer-looking old woman, with brilliant but wicked eyes, and the remains of beauty in her features." She embraced in 1781 the Christian faith, was baptised into the Roman Catholic Church, and christened Johanna Nobilis. This Indian Cleopatra, the Zeb-ul-Nissa, or the ornament of the sex, as designated by her suzerain the Mogul Emperor, died in extreme old age in 1836, and was buried in the beautiful Church which she had erected at her capital of Sirdhana. After her death the principality lapsed to the English.

(5) Petrus Astwasatoor, from Ardzakeek in Armenia.
(6) Lazar Jacob, from the village of Kora in the district of Azerbijan in Persia.
(7) Martyrose Gregory, from the district of Maragah.
(8) Sookeas Avietick, a native of Tabreez in the district of Azerbijan in Persia.
(9) Johanness Nazareth, from Tabreez in Persia.

There is a tombstone in the old cemetery at Chandernagore, bearing an Armenian inscription, which points to the fact that Armenians were engaged in military service before the days of Gorgin Khan. The inscription runs:—

> "This is the tomb of MATTHEW, son of Lazar, the *Commander*. Died on the 8th day of May 1753 A.D."

This takes us back to the days of the prolonged warfare that was waged in Bengal between the Nawab Ali Verdi Khan and the plundering hordes of the formidable Mahrattas. These freebooters frequently invaded Bengal and terrorised the country far and wide. The 'Mahratta Ditch,' or half-finished moat round Calcutta, portions of which still exist, bears record to the panic that had spread throughout Bengal.

Another Armenian who distinguished himself in military service was the renowned Colonel Jacob Petrus, who had command of a division of Scindia's army in the first half of the present century.

He was a native of Erivan in Armenia, and came to India as a needy adventurer in search of his fortune. He found his way to the territories of the famous Mahratta chief, Scindia, the Maharajah of Gwalior, and, entering his military service, gradually rose to the command of a division. His head-quarters were at Gwalior, and a number of Armenians served under him as officers—

commissioned and non-commissioned. In a short time thirty Armenian families settled there.

Some of those who served as officers under Colonel Jacob built up considerable fortunes. One, Mayor Johanness, left a fortune of Rs. 5,00,000; another, Woskan, retired to his native town of Erivan in Armenia, and there enjoyed a life of luxury and ease; a third, John Baptist, erected a magnificent church and a large school at Agra for the benefit of his own people, the Portuguese, to whom he subsequently left the greater portion of his colossal fortune. The battles of Maharajpore and Punniar—which were fought after the death of Janoki Rao Scindia, and during the Governor-Generalship of Lord Ellenborough, between the British and a portion of Scindia's army on the 29th December 1843—resulted in the disbandment of the Maharajah's troops, 'the irrepressible army of 30,000 men'! Most of the Armenians then quitted Gwalior and gave up their martial occupations.

Colonel Jacob was not only an eminent patriot and a true philanthropist, but of a devoutly pious disposition, and his name figured prominently in the pontifical bulls of the Holy See of Etchmiatzin. He erected from his own means an Armenian Church at Gwalior and maintained its Armenian priest at his own expense. He died on 24th June 1850 and his remains were buried at Gwalior. At his funeral, which was largely attended by the nobility and military officers of State, 95 minute guns, equal in number to the years of this veteran, were fired from the ramparts of the Fort. He was held in such high esteem by Scindia of Gwalior, his patron, that the whole city went into mourning at his death. He left a widow, two sons and a daughter. Major Owen Jacob, his son, who succeeded him, was murdered and mutilated by the mutineers at Agra during the Indian Mutiny of 1857. Helen, the pious widow of Colonel Jacob, also died and was buried at Gwalior. Prior to her death she forwarded to the Armenian Church at Calcutta all the sacred vessels and vestments of great intrinsic value which had belonged to the Armenian Church at Gwalior.

In an able article on Indian Numismatics, in the *Journal of the Asiatic Society of Bengal*, vol. lvii., No. 1, of 1888, Mr. Chas. J. Rodgers, Honorary Numismatist to the Government of India, writing of the 'Couplets on Coins after Jahangir,' makes particular mention of the following interesting *bait* on the coins of Shah Shuja, from the pages of the *Tarikh-i-Sultani*, by Sultan Muhammad Khan, son of Musa Khan Durrani. The couplet runs:—

سکه زد بر سیم وطلا شه شجاع ارمني

نور چشم لارڈ برنس خاک پای کمپني

—*i.e.*, "The *Armenian* Shah Shuja, the Light of the Eyes of Lord Burnes, the Dust of the Foot of the Company, put [his] stamp on silver and gold."

Mr. Rodgers remarks that these coins "could never have been struck by the King's permission." It is indeed difficult to understand how they could have been struck at all; for Shah Sujah is distinctly a Muhammadan name.

CHAPTER VII.

BOLTS DENOUNCES THE COMPANY'S POLICY.

THE years 1767-69, as regards the commercial affairs of the Armenian merchants in Bengal, were rather eventful, and I cannot refrain from dwelling upon them at considerable length. We have already seen that, by virtue of a certain Charter, the Armenians were placed in 1688 on an equal footing with the English in India. So long as the East India Company was a purely commercial concern, they enjoyed all its chartered rights and privileges. The Directors had even declared and stipulated

> "That we will not continue any Governor in our service that shall in any kind disturb or discountenance them [the Armenians] in the full enjoyment of all the privileges hereby granted to them, neither shall they pay any other or greater duty in India than the Company's Factors, or any other Englishmen born, do, or ought to do."

Matters took quite a different turn, however, when the Company embarked on territorial power, so as to consolidate its position in India, and was apparently guided by a resolution passed to that effect, which ran as follows :—

> "The increase of our revenue is the subject of our care, as much as our trade; 'tis that must maintain our force when twenty accidents may interrupt our trade, 'tis that must make us a nation in India."

Bolts, who was singularly well informed on Indian affairs, writes :—

"The Armenians, who have ever been a great commercial body in Hindostan, have also long had considerable settlements in Bengal, particularly at Sydabad. Their commerce was likewise established by the Mogul's *firmaun*, whereby the duties on the two principal articles of their trade, piece-goods and raw silk, were fixed at three and one half per cent. But after the subversion of the Mogul empire, and during the reigns of the independent Nabob-usurpers, they, as well as the Europeans, were at times exposed to great impositions, and interruptions of their trade. At present, since the English Company have taken the sovereignty of the country into their own hands, they all trade under the appearance of the old forms, subject in all places within the Bengal provinces, out of the jurisdiction of their respective settlements, to such regulations as the English are pleased to impose on them,* through the nominal Nabobs; which regulations on many occasions amount to a total prohibition of their trade, being in general temporary, contradictory, and wholly calculated for obstruction.

"The difference also between the lawful trade of the Company's servants and that of English free merchants and other persons residing under the Company's production was, that the covenanted servants of the Company, as hath been observed in another place, were, by connivance of the country Government, and long established usage, indulged with *dustucks*† for the carrying on of their trade duty-free; while the others, for want of that *dustuck*, were subjected to the payment of the Government duties. It is true, the inconveniences and impositions, which the want of this *dustuck* exposed the European free-traders to, were such as generally

* When the foreigners prove refractory, the Fowzdar of Hooghly is made to surround their settlements with troops, in the name of *the Nabob*, to stop their provisions, and obstruct their business. This has actually been frequently practised.—*Bolts.*

† An order or passport.

induced them to prefer contracting with the Company's servants for the delivery of such goods as they wanted in Calcutta; and it, in fact, amounted to an almost total exclusion of them from the inland trade, from one place to another, which, when Bengal flourished, was generally very beneficial. With respect to the trade that was actually carried on within the Company's principal settlements of Calcutta, Madras and Bombay, all were, or ought to have been, upon an equal footing.

"Such was the situation of trade before the English Company made themselves the Sovereigns of Bengal; and this representation is agreeable to the ideas of the former Courts of Directors in England, who, in their general letters to India down to the year 1757, and particularly in that year, gave their express sentiments and directions upon this subject to their different presidencies in this manner:—

"'That all persons under the protection of the Company should have the liberty of resorting to, and trading at all and any of the Company's settlements in the East Indies, and at all other places within the Company's limits. in as full, true and extensive a manner as the rest of the Company's servants; they paying the duties, according to the usual and customary methods and rates established at such places.'

"And about the same time, in order to ascertain the rights of persons residing upon the western coast of Sumatra, the Court of Directors were also pleased to give their sentiments to their President and Council at Bombay in the following words:—

"'All persons residing upon the west coast of Sumatra, who shall resort to, or trade either by themselves or their agents, at Fort St. George, Fort William, or Bombay, and their respective dependencies, are to buy and sell publicly or privately, as they themselves shall choose; dealing freely, and without restraint, with whomsoever they shall think proper; and if, contrary to this article, they shall be oppressed or injured by any person whatsoever, such person, or persons, let their rank be what it may, will incur our highest displeasure. and shall certainly feel the weight of our resentment.'

"Those were the judicious orders given for the protection of trade by former Courts of Directors: and by the representation which has been just given to the nature of the English Company's trade in India, the reader, who is a merchant, will easily see that upon a footing of fair trade, it must be ever for the interest of the Company, though not for that of their servants, to encourage private traders of all nations, in India, for these obvious reasons; that the more traders, the more purchasers of the Company's staple imports, the sales of which would be the more industriously pushed in every corner of India; and the more providers of goods at the manufacturing towns, the more the manufacturers would be encouraged, and upon a free inland trade, the more goods would come to market. But since the English East India Company have become the Sovereigns, they and their substitutes have been exclusively the sole merchants of Bengal, and seem to have adopted sentiments as repugnant to the true spirit of mercantile affairs, as could possibly be conceived: nay they have of late even ventured to assert, that they *alone* have a right *to trade in India;* and in consequence of that absurd opinion, they have directed certain merchants, inhabitants of Calcutta, not to trade; alleging, very nicely, that though they may have a legal right to reside at their settlements, they could have no right to trade there; which is the same thing as telling a man he may have a right to live, but no right to use the means of his profession for acquiring the wherewithal to support life.

"It is true that such restrictions have never been laid but upon particular persons whom the Company designed to oppress and crush. But how miserable and despicable must that state of the government of the Company's affairs be, wherein the general system of justice is stopped or perverted, for the sake of oppressing an individual!"

Bolts was perhaps the best authority on the subject, and, in writing "Of the Courts of Law established by the Charter granted to the Company, and of the Government, Police, and Administration of Justice in Bengal," he criticises the policy adopted by the Company's

Governors and Council and their utter disregard of treaty stipulations after the battle of Plassey, when they assumed sovereignty over Bengal. In support of his arguments and criticisms, Bolts cites cases of oppression, violence and miscarriage of justice. For example:—

"One more extraordinary instance we will give of the convenient uses which are made of the Nabobs by the Governor and Council in Calcutta, under whose direction alone they act, whenever it is necessary for any private purpose to oppress individuals; and this is of certain *Armenian merchants* of established credit and reputation, who, like many hundreds of others, had been long established in India, and were at this time peaceably engaged in carrying on their own mercantile business in the dominions bordering on Bengal, which the Company had taken from, and afterwards restored to, the Nabob Sujah-al-Dowlah. The business they carried on greatly interfering with the private views of the Governor and some of the Council at Calcutta and their connections, it was thought necessary to have them removed. Not contented with their being suddenly seized by the Company's troops and confined, without ever being accused, confronted, or heard upon any pretended crime or misbehaviour whatever in the dominions of Sujah-al-Dowlah, the Governor and Council had them brought down into their own provinces, where they could more conveniently manage them, and where they were kept imprisoned for some months, to the utter ruin of themselves and families. After they had been long enough imprisoned to serve the purposes intended, they were set at liberty, but without being acquainted with any reason for such imprisonment: and, despairing of ever obtaining justice in Bengal, two of them came over in quest of it to England; where, flattering themselves that the Court of Directors would naturally discountenance such oppression, they presented a very respectful petition to the Court; which, as it will give the best state of their case, we will present the reader with a copy of, as follows:—

"'*To the* HONOURABLE THE COURT OF DIRECTORS *for the affairs of the Honourable the United Company of Merchants of England, trading to the Indies,*

"'*The Petition of* GREGORE COJAMAUL *and* JOHANNES PADRE RAFAEL, *Armenian Merchants, late of Bengal,*

"'Humbly Sheweth,

"'That your petitioners, who are natives of Ispahan in Persia, have for many years resided in India, particularly in the provinces annexed to Bengal, and in the dominions of the different princes bordering upon those provinces, where they have carried on, for themselves and others, a very extensive trade, always with the permission and approbation of the different princes, in whose dominions your petitioners resided; always paying the duties exacted by such princes, and always cheerfully submitting themselves to the laws of such countries.

"'That it has ever been the custom, from time immemorial, for Greeks, Georgians, Turks, Persians, Tartars, Cashmeerians, Armenians, and other nations, to resort to and traffic in India, where the country Nabobs, sensible of the benefits arising from the resort of foreign merchants and the increase of trade, have at all times encouraged such persons to the utmost of their power.

"'That besides their own traffic, your petitioners likewise, for about seven years last past, have been honoured with business upon commission from sundry English gentlemen, several of whom are now in England.

"'That your petitioners in such transactions have ever acted to the satisfaction of their constituents, and with credit to themselves; having ever studiously avoided interfering in any other than their own mercantile affairs; and they have ever been well-wishers to the Honourable English East India Company, having never, in the most distant manner, acted contrary to the interests of that Company.

"'That your petitioners were lately resident in the dominions of the Nabob Sujah-al-Dowlah,* and the Rajah Bulwant Sing, who, to

* Sujah-al-Dowlah was the Nawab Wazir of Oudh, and, according to Marshman, "the only chief of importance in the north." In November 1763 he had afforded an asylum to Meer Kasim, the expelled and disinherited Nawab of Bengal, and to the notorious Sumru. Actuated by motives of avarice and ambition, he adopted a policy of aggression, marched down at the head of an army of 50 000 men, and on the 3rd of May 1764 laid siege to Patna, where the English army had retired from the field for want of provisions. With great difficulty he was repulsed, and was obliged to retire to Buxar to encamp for the rains. Here on the 23rd October the celebrated victory was gained by Major (afterwards Sir Hector) Munro over the allied forces of Sujah-al-Dowlah and Meer Kasim, who had joined the Nawab Wazir's camp. The battle of Buxar made the English masters of the entire Gangetic valley, and placed the *subah* of Oudh at the feet of the conquerors.

the great surprize of your petitioners, received orders from your Presidency of Calcutta, or Fort William, to banish your petitioners out of their countries.

"'That those princes communicated the orders which they had received from your said Presidency to your petitioners, who had the honour to be favoured with the friendship of the said princes; who proposed various expedients to screen your petitioners from violence, as your petitioners can shew by authentic documents in their hands, to the satisfaction of this Honourable Court.

"'That the friendship of those princes having induced them to evade the immediate execution of such tyrannical orders, for which they knew no cause, your President Mr. Verelst wrote again in repeated letters, and in most peremptory terms, to have your petitioners seized, imprisoned and sent down into the Company's provinces to Patna and Murshedabad; and for fear of further delays or evasions, orders were given to the immediate servants of the English Company, who were employed to seize and imprison your petitioners, as they are likewise ready to prove to the satisfaction of this Honourable Court, by authentic documents and writings under the hands and seals of the said Company's servants.

"'That accordingly your petitioners were seized in the most sudden, cruel and inhuman manner, and brought down to the Company's factories at Patna and Murshedabad, being obliged to quit instantly all they were possessed of in that country, to a very considerable amount, together with their books and papers, and the effects of many other persons with which they were intrusted, and for which they are accountable.

"'That during the confinement of your petitioners, their relations did deliver to your President, Mr. Harry Verelst, sundry petitions, particularly one of the 15th May 1768, and one of the 13th June 1768 (which your petitioners imagine stand recorded upon your Calcutta consultations), requesting the releasement of your petitioners, and offering to give any such security for money, or the appearance of your petitioners, as might appear reasonable to your said President and Council.

"'That the said petitions were paid no regard to, but your petitioners were continued under confinement; your petitioner *Gregore Cojamaul* having been confined from the 14th March 1768 to the 23rd May 1768, being two months and nine days; and your petitioner *Johannes Padre Rafael*, from the 27th March 1768 to the 28th August 1768, being five months; during which time they were treated worse than convicted felons: Cogee [Khojah] Rafael being first imprisoned in a horse-stable, and afterwards both kept in close confinement under a strong guard of the Company's seapoys, with fixed bayonets, who never suffered your petitioners to stir out of their sight.

"'That being at last released from confinement, your petitioners and their friends waited upon your President, Mr. Harry Verelst, not only to be acquainted what were the causes of his displeasure, and why they had been confined, but requesting leave to return up the country to secure their effects and outstanding concerns, thereby to preserve themselves and families from ruin; but, to the misfortune of your petitioners, all their applications were paid no regard to, nor could they ever obtain any satisfaction, or be acquainted why they had been thus conspicuously imprisoned for so long a time, and then set at liberty, without being accused of even a fictitious misdemeanor?

"'That, to the great astonishment of your petitioners, upon their arrival in Calcutta, they were informed, that your Governor, Mr. Harry Verelst, and his Council had been pleased to publish an edict, under date of the 18th May 1768, prohibiting all Armenians, Portuguese and their descendants, *from residing or trading in any part* OUT *of the provinces of Bengal, Bahar and Orissa, or attempting to transport any merchandise beyond those provinces, under penalty of the utmost severe corporal punishment, and the confiscation of such merchandize;* an attested notorial copy of which most extraordinary public edict [*see* p. 90] is in the hands of your petitioners, for the inspection of this Honourable Court.

"'That your petitioners were hereby not only deprived, among others, of those rights which were due to them, as men, by the law of nations, but were deprived of that freedom of trade which their nation had always enjoyed in the times of the worst of the ancient BLACK NABOBS, and in particular were also deprived of all hopes of ever recovering those effects from which they had been thus forcibly and capriciously taken.

"'That your petitioners, who have been therefore necessitated at a great expense to come to England for justice, now appeal to the equity of this Honourable Court; requesting, that they will either indemnify your petitioners from the great losses they sustain, or that they will be pleased to order home, to answer for themselves, the President Mr. Verelst, and such of the Company's servants as to this Honourable Court may appear to have been the acting persons in the oppressions complained of.

"'And your petitioners, as in duty bound, shall ever pray.

(Sd.) "'GREGORE COJAMAUL *

(„) "'JOHANNES PADRE RAFAEL. †

"'London, the 12th September 1769.'"

---

* I find in an Armenian book, printed in 1788 at St Petersburg, that Gregore Cojamaul had, after a stay of ten years in London, gone over to St. Petersburg and there started an Armenian press, the *first* in that metropolis. He had the type cast for the same while at London, "and that at a great cost" it having been his cherished desire from his youth upwards to start a new press. His death at the Russian capital must have occurred before 1788, the year in which the book was printed "at the press of the *late* Mr. Gregore, son of Cojamaul, of the family of Khaldareantz."

† It was this Khojah Rafael who in 1775 sold the celebrated Indian diamond to Prince Orloff, whom he met at Amsterdam, *en route* for Russia.

Bolts, who, in his official capacity as an "Alderman or Judge of the Honourable the Mayor's Court of Calcutta," knew but too well of the high-handed policy of the Governor and Council of Calcutta, and of the want of equity of the Honourable the Court of Directors, makes the following observation regarding the above petition:—

"It was natural for these injured Armenian merchants, who then knew but little of the state of the Company and the party views of its Directors, to imagine that the Court would have shewn some readiness, if not a serious disposition, to redress their wrongs. But, to their [the Court of Directors'] shame be it spoken! the petition is said to have been thrown aside, and to have lain by, unanswered and disregarded to this day;* while these *foreign gentlemen*, as is said, have been left to seek redress at law, exactly in the distressful situation already described; exposed to the necessity of sending commis-

---

This historical diamond, which once formed one of the eyes of the celebrated Hindu idol in Srirangum, a fortified island in Mysore, is now set in the Russian Imperial sceptre immediately beneath the Golden Eagle. It weighs 194¾ carats, has the underside flat, and is named after Prince Orloff, its purchaser. Mr. Edwin W Streeter in his *Great Diamonds of the World*, says:—"It was on his way from England to Russia that Khojeh [Rafael] met Prince Orloff in Amsterdam, and induced him to purchase the Indian gem for his mistress, the Czarina, Catherine II. Orloff was himself at the time also on his travels. Having fallen under the displeasure of Catherine, he had absented himself from Court until the storm should blow over. Khojeh's offer was now eagerly accepted, as affording an excellent opportunity for recovering the favour of the Empress, who is reported to have already declined the purchase as too costly, but who now accepted the jewel at the hands of her illustrious subject. Orloff paid the merchant £90,000 in cash, besides procuring him an annuity of £4 000. According to some accounts a patent of nobility was added." Mirza Abu Taleb Khan, the Persian traveller, who met Khojah Rafael at Leghorn, describes him as one "who had seen a great deal of the world, and understood a number of languages. He had left Persia when a young man, and had gone by sea to Surat; thence across the Peninsula to Bengal. After residing there some time, he made a voyage to England; and after travelling over a great part of Europe, at length settled as a merchant in Leghorn." (*Travels in Asia, Africa, and Europe*: London, 1814, vol. II., p. 301.)

* That is, the year 1772 when he published in London his *Considerations on India Affairs*, from which the above is an extract.

sions to India for evidence, and of waiting for the precarious arrival of their oppressors from India; some of whom may perhaps shamelessly attempt to screen themselves by the practised and now usual subterfuge, of pretending the matter complained of was transacted by THE NABOB, in the extra-judicial districts of the charter.

"Many other instances might be given to prove the badness of the Government, Police, and administration of justice in those distant dominions; some of which, though there looked upon as trifles, would in this country be considered as matters of the most serious consequence. Indeed, to enumerate all the facts of that nature which have come within the writer's knowledge would be to fill a large folio volume. It would, moreover, be a task shocking to humanity; and as it is presumed sufficient have already been produced to convince the reader of the truth of our assertions upon the subject-matter of this chapter, we shall hasten to a conclusion of it."

The edict referred to in the petition of the two injured Armenian merchants, issued at Calcutta by the Governor and Council, ran thus:—

"'Fort William, 18th May 1768.

"'Notice is hereby given that, after the expiration of Two Months, from the 27th April, no *gomastahs* employed by the English shall be permitted to remain in any part *out* of the provinces of Bengal, Bahar, and Orissa; and after that period, that no Company's servant, free merchant, or other European residing under the Company's protection, shall be suffered to carry on any inland trade, directly or indirectly, *beyond* those limits, under penalty, if a Company's servant, of being immediately dismissed the service; if a free merchant, or other European, of forfeiting the Company's protection: and that, if any Europeans whatsoever shall attempt to transport any merchandize *beyond* the provinces, all such merchandize shall be seized and confiscated, and the *gomastahs*, having charge of such contraband trade, shall be punished with the utmost severity

"'All Armenians, Portuguese, or the descendants of Armenians and Portuguese, living under the Company's protection, are included in the above restrictions. It being intended that none but *the natives* of the country (Mussulmen and Hindoos) shall in future enjoy this privilege.

"'SIMEON DROZ, Secretary.'

"'I. John Holme, Notary Publick, dwelling and practising at Calcutta at Fort William in Bengal, do hereby certify and attest, that the within writing is a true copy of a paper affixed to the door of the Town-Hall of Calcutta aforesaid, carefully collated by me with the original, exhibited to me for that purpose.

"'In faith and testimony whereof, I have hereunto set my hand and seal, at Calcutta, the first day of July, in the year of our Lord one thousand seven hundred and sixty eight.

(Sd.) ''JOHN HOLME, Notary Publick.'"

Bolts makes the following comments on the edict :—

"To particularize, in a mercantile community, all the gross absurdities and the injustice of such an order, would be to offer an insult to every man of understanding; we will therefore only remark, that this order principally contributed to the producing of two ruinous effects; one, the prevention of extending the Company's sales of British woollens and other staple commodities of this kingdom, and the other, adding to the discouragement of the inland importation of bullion, by lessening all mercantile connections with the merchants of the interior parts of Hindoostan. From whence the Company, or their Governor and Council, could derive these powers of confiscation and punishment, or by what authority they could deprive of their natural rights, the Armenians and Portugueze established in Bengal, who, as well as their forefathers, were natives of that country equally with the *Mussulmen and Hindoos;* or with what view they wanted to prevent all trade in the dominions bordering upon Bengal, notwithstanding the Princes of such adjacent countries permitted, encouraged, and, according to *the usages of the empire,* could not prevent such trade, it must be hard to account for, unless from *private selfish motives;* which latter we are the more inclined to believe must have been the case, as the gentlemen who made this restrictive order also continued their own agents and *gomastahs* in the interdicted districts."

CHAPTER VIII.

MONOPOLY OF SALT, BETEL-NUT, AND TOBACCO.

DURING the eventful years 1760-64, which saw the fall of the Nawab Meer Jafir, and the rise, revolt, and rout of his substitute, the formidable Nawab Meer Kasim, the affairs of the Company were in a chaotic state of disorder and mismanagement. The Company were the actual rulers and Nawab-makers of Bengal; and Clive had during his first able Governorship (1758-60) indicated no proper system of Government in Bengal, but merely, as Hunter remarks, "the tradition that unlimited sums of money might be extracted from the natives by the terror of the English name," a policy which was followed many a time and oft.

Clive was absent in England from 1760 to 1765. In a long and important letter to the Hon'ble the Court of East India Directors, dated "Berkeley Square, the 27th April 1764," proposing to return to Bengal as Governor of the Company's settlements, he, after mature deliberation, gave them, among other things, his opinion with reference to the troubles in connection with the revolt of Nawab Meer Kasim, to the following effect:—

"That it was the encroachments made upon the *Nabob's prescriptive rights*, by the Governor and Council, and the rest of the servants in Bengal trading in the articles of salt, beetle-nut and tobacco, which had greatly contributed to hasten and bring on the troubles with Nabob Cossim Ally Khawn. That, therefore, as the trading in salt, beetle-nut and tobacco had been one cause of the disputes which then had subsisted, his Lordship hoped those articles would be restored to the Nabob, and the Company's servants absolutely forbid to trade in them. This would be striking at the root of the evil, tend to restore that economy which was so necessary in the service of the Company, and serve to prevent the sudden acquisition of fortunes that had of late taken place, and which, if not put a stop to, the Company's affairs must greatly suffer. And his Lordship promised, as a means to alleviate in some measure the dissatisfaction that such restrictions upon the commercial advantages of the Company's servants might occasion in them, *that he would not engage in any kind of trade himself*, but leave all commercial advantages (the Governor's portion of which used to be always very considerable) to the servants to be divided amongst themselves."

Lord Clive's favourable representations to the East India Directors, and his professions of disinterestedness, although feigned, produced the desired effect, and his Lordship was accordingly nominated a second time by the Court of Directors to the Government of Bengal.

Clive, now Baron Clive of Plassey in the peerage of Ireland, arrived at Calcutta, on 23rd June 1765, as Governor of Bengal. He held that high appointment until 1767, and discharged his onerous duties in such an able and statesmanlike manner that he succeeded in placing the Indian administration on what was then considered to be a sound and firmer basis—a task of considerable magnitude, viewed from a diplomatic standpoint.

Among the many reforms which Clive introduced and successfully carried through during his second Governorship, the re-organization of the Company's Service deserves more than a passing notice. By way of encouragement, the Company's servants had been allowed the lucrative privilege of trading privately on their own account, in order to add to their legal salaries, which were rather paltry. Clive, in his zeal to purify the Service from the common corruption which was rather prejudicial to the interests of the Company, strictly prohibited them from continuing private trade, and endeavoured to stamp out their illicit gains in the shape of gifts and presents to them from native chiefs and rulers; but as a recompense, their salaries were largely augmented, the increase being provided out of the *monopoly of salt.* By this monopoly the trade of the Armenian merchants in that commodity was seriously affected, and they were subjected at times to acts of violence and oppression at the hands of the monopolists. Clive is said to have been mainly actuated by considerations of private interest and gain in promoting the monopoly, in which he held a large share: the provision for the Company's servants out of it was merely a subterfuge.

Bolts with his impartial criticism "On the late Monopoly of Salt, Beetle-nut and Tobacco," strongly comments upon it:—

"We come now to consider a monopoly the most cruel in its nature, and most destructive in its consequences, to the Company's affairs in Bengal, of all that have of late been established there. Perhaps it stands unparalleled in the history of any government that ever existed on earth, considered as a public act; and we shall be not less astonished when we consider the men who promoted it, and the reasons given by them for the establishment of such exclusive dealings in what may there be considered as necessaries of life."

On Clive's representations, the Court of Directors were pleased to sanction the restoration of the trade in salt, beetle-nut and tobacco to the Nawab, and accordingly they appointed a Select Committee, "consisting of his Lordship, Mr. William Brightwell Sumner, Brigadier-General Carnac, also Messrs. Harry Verelst and Francis Sykes, with full powers to pursue whatever means they should judge most proper, to attain the desirable ends of restoring and establishing peace and tranquillity in Bengal." But Bolts tells us that "the Committee soon lost sight of the orders and intentions of the Court of Directors, and, in contradiction to his Lordship's most solemn declarations, a universal public monopoly of those three articles was determined on: the profits of which were to be divided among themselves, and such others of the Company's servants as they thought proper."

At a meeting of the Select Committee, held on the 10th August 1765 at Fort William, "to take under their consideration the subject of the inland trade in the articles of salt, beetle-nut and tobacco," several resolutions were passed, and a notification, which shews the mode adopted for carrying them into execution, was published in different languages and posted up in several parts of the town, of which the following is a true copy:—

ADVERTISEMENT.

"The Honourable the Court of Directors having thought proper to send out particular orders for *limiting* the inland trade, in the articles of salt, beetle-nut and tobacco, the same is now to be carried on. *in conformity to those orders*, by a public society of proprietors, to be formed for that purpose; and an exclusive right to the trade of those articles will be vested *in this society, by an authority derived from the Company and from* THE NABOB; all manner of persons dependent upon the Honourable Company's Government are hereby strictly prohibited from dealing in any respect, directly or indirectly, in the articles of salt, beetle-nut or tobacco, from the date hereof; that is to say, that they shall not enter into any new engagements, unless as contractors, either for the purchase or sale of those articles, with the society of trade."

With reference to this odious monopoly, Bolts acquaints us with the fact that

"The Court of East India Directors repeatedly, and in the strongest terms, forbade this monopoly in salt, beetle-nut and tobacco; and particularly in their General Letter to Bengal per the *Lord Camden*, dated the 19th February 1766, wherein they positively directed their Governor and Council to make a formal renunciation by some solemn act to be entered on their records, of all right to trade in those articles; directing their said Presidency to transmit such renunciation in form *to the Nabob*, in the Persian language, with adding these express words:

"'Whatever Government may be established, or whatever unforeseen occurrences may arise, it is our resolution to prohibit, and we do absolutely forbid this trade in salt. beetle-nut and tobacco.'

"In all their subsequent letters they continued to repeat this prohibition, giving as their sentiments, that 'such innovations and illegal traffic had laid the foundation of all the bloodshed, massacres and confusion which had happened in Bengal.'"

In one of his letters to the Court of East India Directors, Clive, who was the moving spirit in the establishment of the monopoly, said that it was not an *unprecedented thing*, in proof whereof he mentioned that:—

"It is an erroneous opinion, that salt was formerly an open trade; it ever was, *and ever must be*, a monopoly. Some great favourite, or favourites, always had the whole in their own hands, for which he not only paid an annual *Peshcush*, or acknowledgment in money to the Subah, but likewise gave considerable presents both in money and curiosities to him and to his ministers."

The 'great favourite' referred to by Clive was the Armenian Khojah Wazeed, concerning whom Bolts gives the following information:—

"In the time of the Nabob *Allaverdy Khawn*, his favourite, Cogee [Khojah] Wazeed, was irregularly allowed to farm the trade in salt: but that merchant sold his salt then *five hundred per cent. cheaper* than it was sold after the establishment by this Committee of the monopoly now under consideration. In many parts of Bengal, Cogee [Khojah] Wazeed used to sell his salt for *forty, fifty, or sixty* Rupees *per hundred Maunds;* and at Patna, before this monopoly took place, at one time the market price of salt was so low as *one hundred and fifty* Rupees *per hundred Maunds.* After this monopoly was established, salt was sold in many parts of Bengal for upwards of *three hundred* Rupees *per hundred Maunds*, and in some parts of the Patna province it was raised to upwards of *eight hundred and fifty* Rupees *per hundred Maunds.*"

Marshman, in his *History of Bengal*, writes regarding this monopoly and Khojah Wazeed's perfidy to the Nawab:—

"Khojah Wajeed was a great favourite of Alivardi Khan and had possessed a monopoly of the trade in salt. He had become so exceedingly wealthy, that his daily expenditure was a thousand rupees, and he on one occasion presented fifteen lakhs of rupees to the Nawab. He had formerly been the Agent of the French at Moorshedabad, but when their power was destroyed by the fall of Chandernagore, he came over to the English. Sirajooddowlah placed great confidence in him; yet he was the principal actor in inviting the English to depose that Nawab."

This odious monopoly, at its initiation, was conducted in a violently oppressive and highly arbitrary manner:—

"Upon the establishment of the private copartnership, or society, of the gentlemen of the Committee among themselves, there was an Armenian merchant, named Parseek Arratoon, who had about 20,000 maunds of salt lying in warehouses upon the borders of the Rungpore and Dinagepore provinces. The Armenian, sensible, as well as the gentlemen of the Committee, that the price of salt would rise, ordered his *gomastah* to fasten up his warehouses, and not to sell. As the retailing of this salt in those parts might hurt the partnership's sales, it was thought expedient, at any rate, if possible, to get possession of it. Upon failure of the artifices which were practised to induce the *gomastah* to sell it, the Armenian merchant's warehouses were broke open, the salt forcibly taken out and weighed off, and a sum of money, estimated to be the price of it, was forced upon the Armenian's *gomastah*, on his refusing to receive it. Such are the facts sworn to in the depositions of several witnesses, upon an action, or bill of complaint filed in the Mayor's Court of Calcutta, the 15th September 1767, by Parseek Arratoon, plaintiff, against the *gomastahs* or agents of Messrs. Verelst and Sykes, for current rupees 60,432, and if the proceedings of the Mayor's Court have been transmitted home with the same punctual regularity as formerly, there must be sufficient proof of these facts among the records now in Leaden Hall Street."*

Parseek Arratoon appealed to the equity of the Honourable Company's Courts, by filing a suit in the Mayor's Court against the unwarrantable conduct of the agents of the Governor Harry Verelst and Francis Sykes. Justice would have been administered in his case, had the said Governor, whose interests were at stake and at whose instance the oppression was committed, not arbitrarily put a stop to the proceedings in a most unjustifiable manner. Bolts, however, took up the matter. He writes concerning it:—

"We now come to the exemplification of what we have advanced, by real facts, in which the writer will either confine himself to matters of which he himself hath perfect knowledge, and can even produce proof, or to such others as appear well vouched by authentic documents exhibited in different parts of this work; and we will begin with the Mayor's Court.

---

* Bolts' *Considerations on Indian Affairs.*

"In consequence of a most extraordinary oppression in the inland parts of the country, of which particular notice is taken in our 13th chapter, an Armenian merchant, named Parseek Arratoon, on the 15th September 1767, filed a bill in the Mayor's Court against the *gomastahs* or agents of Governor Harry Verelst and Francis Sykes, Esquires, for 60,432 current rupees or about 7,500 pounds sterling, principal amount of salt, said to have been forcibly taken out of the plaintiff's warehouses. The cause was brought to an issue; and in the month of August 1768, on a day appointed for the hearing, all the proceedings and depositions were read and fully considered; the demand of the plaintiff established to all appearance, and judgment upon the point of being pronounced, when the Mayor, while sitting in judgment, received a private letter * or note, sent from the Governor, to put a stop to the proceedings, because, as was alledged, he, the said Governor, was a party concerned in the cause, and was in expectation of settling matters by a private compromise. To the astonishment of the plaintiff's solicitor, who declared he knew of no compromise, and had received no instructions from his client upon this matter, the request contained in the letter or note was complied with, and a stop was at once put to the proceedings; the plaintiff being left without any satisfaction.

"After an instance of this sort, it may be thought needless to produce others of a less criminal nature.

---

* "The writer of these sheets being an Alderman of the Court, and having been absent when this extraordinary transaction happened, as soon as he heard of it, wrote to the Mayor upon the subject, desiring to have a sight of the letter sent by, or by the order of, the Governor, then Harry Verelst, Esquire, in consequence of which the proceedings had been stopped. After some days' consideration, the Mayor wrote the following excuse, the original of which is now in the writer's possession:—

"'To WILLIAM BOLTS, Esquire.

"'Dear Sir,—I shou'd have sent you the note. as I promised, if I had found it; but having n t met with it among my papers, convinces me that I must have destroyed it, with other papers th t I *deemed useless.*

I am, Sir, Your most obedient servant,
CORNELIUS GOODWIN.

"'Calcutta, the 11th August 1768.'"—*Bolts.*

But it is notorious in Calcutta, that in cases wherein the said Governor and Council, or those of their connections, have been any wise interested, private applications, by letter or otherwise, have been frequently received by the Court; who, setting aside the formalities of process as directed by the Charter, have actually proceeded to hear and determine upon such private applications, particularly against the attorneys or solicitors of the Court, who have found it a hazardous matter to undertake any suit in matters of arbitrary proceedings, wherein the Governor and Council have been in the least degree interested separately or collectively."

We have already seen that the Court of Directors strictly prohibited, since its commencement, the monopoly in salt, betel-nut and tobacco; but, as communication with England was very slow in those days, the monopoly continued for two years before it was finally put a stop to by the Directors at home. There were sixty shares in the concern, and the shareholders, who were the rulers of the country, had during that short period made a profit of Rs. 1,074,002! That the monopoly was highly profitable, may also be inferred from the fact that on one occasion two wealthy native merchants of Calcutta, who were accused of having sold salt at other prices than that fixed by the monopolists, were fined to the amount of Rs. 40,000.

In a subsequent chapter, "On the General Modern Trade of the English in Bengal; on the Oppressions and Monopolies which have been the causes of the decline of Trade, the Decrease of the Revenues, and the Present Ruinous Condition of Affairs in Bengal," the same author, writing of the oppressions consequent on the enforcement of other monopolies, mentions, among others, the following instances, in which the peaceable Armenians were the injured parties and sufferers, in defiance of treaty obligations and solemn stipulations on the part of the Honourable Company:—

"With every species of monopoly, therefore, every kind of oppression to manufacturers, of all denominations throughout the whole country, has daily increased; insomuch that weavers, for daring to sell their goods, and *dallals* and *pykars*, for having contributed to or connived at such sales, have, by the Company's agents, been frequently seized and imprisoned, confined in irons, fined considerable sums of money, flogged, and deprived, in the most ignominious manner, of what they esteem most valuable, their castes. Weavers also, upon their inability to perform such agreements as have been forced from them by the Company's agents, universally known in Bengal by the name of *Mutchulcahs*, have had their goods seized, and sold on the spot, to make good the deficiency: and the winders of raw silk, called *Nagaads*, have been treated also with such injustice, that instances have been known of their cutting off their thumbs, to prevent their being forced to wind silk. This last kind of workmen were pursued with such rigour during Lord Clive's late government in Bengal, from a zeal for increasing the Company's investment of raw silk, that the most sacred laws of society were atrociously violated; for it was a common thing for the Company's seapoys to be sent by force of arms to break open the houses of the Armenian merchants established at Sydabad (who have, from time immemorial, been largely concerned in the silk trade) and forcibly take the *Nagaads* from their work, and carry them away to the English factory."

In the same chapter the author observes:—

"The public monopoly next in consequence, as of late practised, has been that of piece-goods fit for the markets of Bussorah, Judda, Mocha, Bombay, Surat and Madrass. Of those goods there are many sorts which the English Company do not deal in, such as, at Dacca, the coarser kinds of Mulmuls, called Anundy, Hyaty,

Sonargoung and Sherbetty; and at Cossimbazar and Radnagore several sorts of Sarries, called Chappa, Mugga, Tempy, Tarachaundy and Mucta; also Soocies and Soocy-Sarries, Cuttanees and Tasseties, &c., in the provision of which nevertheless, under the same influence, like oppressions are practised as for the Company's investment.

"For the disposal of the goods of this joint concern, another monopoly is established of the exclusive right of exportation, particularly to Bussorah, Judda and Mocha, which used to be the most profitable voyages. For this purpose, the Governor and Council of Calcutta fit out ships, generally known by the denomination of the Freight Ships, on which the goods of this joint concern are first shipped, and the remainder of the tonnage is fitted up on freight. The management of this concern is under the direction of a member of the Council, who is acting-owner, and keeps a warehouse for this purpose, generally known in Calcutta by the name of the Freight Warehouse. When one of these freight-ships is set up, no other persons among the few that can provide goods dare attempt to set up another on the same voyage, without the permission of the Governor and Council; nor is any person suffered to load their goods on any other ship for those markets, if such should be permitted to be set up, until the loading of the freight-ship of the Governor and Council be completed. Frequent instances have been known of the goods of private merchants, even Europeans, but particularly of those belonging to Armenians, Moguls and Gentoos,* being, in consequence of this monopoly, stopped on the public road, and by force carried to the freight-warehouse; and the proprietors of such goods have been obliged, contrary to their

* *Gentoo* is a Portuguese word, meaning *Gentiles* in the Biblical parlance. By this general appellation they at first called all the natives of India, whether Hindoos or Muhammadans, and from them the English adopted the term *Gentoo*—an appellation by which they distinguished the Hindoos, as followers of Brahma, from the Muhammadans or Musalmans, whom they commonly, though improperly, called *Moors*, or *Moormen*.

wills, to see their goods shipped on vessels they had not a good opinion of, and going on voyages whose destination and management were often contrary to their own private schemes of trade: in consequence of which unwarrantable proceedings, those merchants have frequently lost their sales, have had their goods damaged, left at ports they never designed they should touch at, and have sometimes lost even the goods themselves. By all which cruel circumstances there have been in Bengal many instances of families of Armenians, principal traders in this branch to Persia and Arabia, the former of which may properly be called their own country, who have been *totally ruined.*"

CHAPTER IX.

TWO ARMENIANS OF WEALTH AND HONOUR.

THE Armenian Church of St. Nazareth, in Calcutta, which had been repaired and embellished in 1763 by Khojah Petrus Arratoon, was considerably improved in 1790 by Agah Catchick Arrakiel, a prominent member of the Armenian community of Calcutta. He had the church compound surrounded by a substantial wall, and built the present parsonage within the enclosure. He also presented the church with a valuable English clock, which, although it has measured time for over a century on the belfry attached to the church, is still considered to be one of the best in Calcutta.

In the second volume of *Selections from the 'Calcutta Gazettes' of the years 1789-1797*, published in 1865 under the sanction of the Government of India, there is (page 220) an account of the great rejoicing and festivities in Calcutta in July 1788, on hearing the happy news that George III. had recovered from his unfortunate malady. The writer, after giving a full and descriptive account of the proceedings on the part of the Government and all classes of the population, concludes :—

"We cannot pass over in the occurrences of Tuesday, the liberality of a Lady of the settlement who presented a thousand rupees to be distributed by the Committee for the relief of debtors in such manner as they judged most beneficial.

"Another instance of liberality was also exhibited by Mr. Catchick Arrakiel, a wealthy Armenian merchant and an old inhabitant of this settlement, who liberated, at his own expense, all the debtors confined by the Court of Requests * to the number of sixteen. This act of generosity cost Mr. Catchick Arrakiel, as we understood, three thousand rupees. This gentleman and many other Armenians illuminated their houses and church in the most splendid manner."

The East India Company brought this noble act to the King's kind notice, and, as a mark of royal approbation, he was graciously pleased to present Mr. Arrakiel with his miniature portrait and a valuable sword. Perhaps no higher honour would be conferred by a king on a humble subject. But Agah Catchick Arrakiel had departed this life, at the early age of forty-eight years, on 25th July 1790, before the royal gifts reached Calcutta, and they were therefore presented to his eldest son, Agah Moses Catchick Arrakiel, by the Governor-General, the Marquis of Cornwallis, at a public *levée* in Government House. They have since remained as heir-looms in the family. The writer has had the great pleasure of handling the miniature portrait, which is now in the possession of a distant member of the Arrakiel family residing in Calcutta. It is a bust, in miniature, of the

* "The third Court is the Court of Requests, consisting of twenty-four Commissioners, selected originally by the Governor and Council from among the principal inhabitants of Calcutta, who are appointed by the said charter to sit every Thursday, with powers to hear and determine suits in a summary way. under such orders and regulations as shall from time to time be given by a majority of the Court of East India Directors; which Commissioners, or any three or more of them, are to sit in rotation, and have full power and authority to determine all such actions or suits as shall be brought before them, where the debt or matter in dispute shall not exceed the value of five pagodas, or forty shillings. One half of the number of the Commissioners. being those who have longest served, are removed by rotation annually, on the first Thursday of December, and an equal number are chosen by ballot from among themselves."—*Bolts.*

august sovereign, King George III., neatly painted on a thin plate of ivory, and mounted in a substantial gold frame. The whole is surmounted by a small crown in gold, and is suspended by a gold chain long enough to go round the neck, as is customary with medallions, &c.

The following obituary notice, which appeared in the *Calcutta Gazette* on 29th July 1790, portrays the character of Mr. Arrakiel and depicts the great esteem in which he was held:—

"The 29th July 1790.

"On Sunday last, in the morning of the 25th instant, departed this life that truly respectable and worthy character, Mr. Catchick Arrakiel, an Armenian merchant of the first rank and eminence in Calcutta and the head and principal of the Armenian nation in Bengal.

"The goodness, humanity, and benevolence of this man towards all mankind, his liberal spirit in contributing to the public welfare on every occasion, the affability of his deportment and friendly disposition to all, were distinguished traits of his character; he was so warmly and gratefully attached to the English nation, that he was continually heard to express his happiness and a sense of his fortunate lot in being under their Government. He possessed the regard of the whole settlement, unsullied by the enmity of a single individual. Among his own beloved nation, the Armenians, he was looked up to as a guide and director in all their difficulties and disputes, which he was ever studious to settle with paternal affection.

"The inward satisfaction of doing good and love to God, were the sole motives which governed this virtuous man in the exercise of his charity and benevolence, without any mixture of vanity or ostentation.

"He has left a disconsolate widow and a numerous family of seven children, whom he most tenderly loved. He died lamented, not only by his own nation, but by all the different sects in Bengal, and especially by the

Greeks, to whom he rendered the most essential service. In short, no individual ever died more universally regretted, or whose loss will be longer and more sincerely felt.

"To this good man, without the smallest deviation from truth, may be applied the Scriptural character given to Job (chap. xxix):—

"'I was a father to the poor, and the cause which I knew not I searched out. I was eyes to the blind and feet to the lame.

"'I put on righteousness, and it clothed me. My judgment was a robe and a diadem. Then I said I shall die in my rest, and I shall multiply my days as the stars of the firmament.'

"Mr. Catchick Arrakiel was born in Upper Armenia, and died in the forty-eighth year of his age; he was descended from a very respectable family; one of his immediate ancestors was Cazee [Khojah] Phanoos Calendar [Khalanthar],* who was greatly distinguished about a century ago for his zeal and attachment to the English, and by whose conduct and management the English East India Company was induced to grant several beneficial commercial privileges to the Armenians either trading in or to India.

"His remains were interred on Sunday morning, between ten and eleven o'clock in the Armenian church after the celebration of High Mass. The funeral was attended by a very numerous and respectable company; the Armenian Bishops with all the clergy of the same church; Colonel Fullarton and two Aides-de-Camp of the Right Hon'ble the Governor-General with many other gentlemen, Civil and Military."

In him the Armenian community of Calcutta lost their respected head and leader. His remains were honoured by being buried inside their church, where his tombstone may be seen bearing an inscription in Armenian, surmounted by the figure of a rider on a fiery steed

---

* From researches this year (1895) in the archives of the East India House, London, by Professor Wilson of Calcutta, it appears that the Armenian Khojah Sarhad, who in 1715 obtained the *Grand Firman* for the English, was a nephew of Khojah Phanoos Khalanthar.

in bold relief, emblematic of an angel, holding in his right hand a spear and in the left a pair of scales, symbolic of righteousness. In 1837, a black marble mural tablet was erected by the Armenian community of Calcutta in their church of St. Nazareth as a tribute to his memory. His widow survived him thirty-five years, and her remains were placed next to those of her husband.

With reference to the obituary notice, telling us that Agah Catchick Arrakiel's loss was keenly felt not only by the Armenians, but by men of other nationalities, "and especially by the *Greeks*, to whom he rendered the most essential service," it is a known fact that the early Greek settlers in Calcutta always relied upon the patronage of the influential Armenian merchants. In this connection it will be interesting to give a sketch of the history of the Greeks in India.

The Greeks, under Alexander the Great, invaded India in 327 B.C., but did not found a kingdom here. They left traces, however, of their knowledge of astronomy, and specimens of their exquisite sculptures made in India may be seen in Indian museums. The invasion, nevertheless, was of great historical importance; for India to the east of the Indus was first made known to Europe by the historians and men of science who accompanied Alexander to India.

It is somewhat strange that the Greeks, who were acquainted with this country since the dawn of history, did not return to India after the days of Antiochos, a contemporary of Asoka, the famous Buddhist king. Not until the middle of the eighteenth century do we again find Greeks in India, where commerce had allured them in the train of foreign traders. The Armenians then represented the leading commercial element of Calcutta and carried on a lucrative trade under the protection and auspices of the English East India Company, with whom they were in the highest degree of favour.

The Greek settlers saw the advisability of attaching themselves to their brother-traders, the Armenians, for fear of being ousted by other rival traders of influence. They cultivated the friendships and solicited the patronage of the Armenians. Both were generously accorded them. The Greeks entered into an agreement with the Armenians, in terms of which they paid into the Armenian Church of St. Nazareth, Calcutta, the sum of *one Arcot rupee* on every bale of merchandise that they brought down to Calcutta from Murshidabad, Dacca, Sylhet, Assam, Patna and Bandana. This fact affords the strongest proof of their being under a deep debt of gratitude to the Armenians.

To return to the subject-matter. Contemporary with Agah Catchick Arrakiel, there lived in Calcutta Massy Baba John, whose name is here worthy of record for his philanthropy and patriotism. Not unlike many of his eminent countrymen, he belonged to the 'self-made' class of men. His birthplace was the historical city of Hamadan* in Persia. Leaving his native town in early

* Hamadan, a town of historical interest in Persia, lies in a low plain at the foot of Mount Elwand in Irak Ajemi on the high road from Bagdad to Teheran and Ispahan. On its site, or near it stood the far-famed Ecbatana, the ancient capital of Media, founded according to Herodotus by Deioces, who delivered the Medes from the yoke of the Assyrians and in 700 B.C. ascended the throne of Media. Ecbatana was the favourite residence of the Persian kings during the summer (Susa during the winter). It is said to have been destroyed by Nebuchadnezzar, king of Ninevah and Babylon, and rebuilt by Darius. Ecbatana is mentioned in the Bible in connection with the patriotic deeds of Esther, the Jewish Queen of the Persian king, Ahaserius (Artaxerxes). The revered shrines of Esther and Mordechai, which are in the custody of the Jews, can be seen to this day at the city of Hamadan, where there are many Jews. The Armenians settled there in the reign of the Great Shah Abbas, the Sefavi king of Persia.

life, he came to India and settled permanently in Calcutta, where he was a respectable citizen and an eminent merchant. He became the happy possessor of a large fortune, of which more hereafter. His last will and testament was made out on the 30th day of May 1794, in the Armenian language, and an important codicil, under date the 1st day of April 1795, was added to it, true copies of which I have in my possession. That he was animated by a noble spirit of piety, is evinced by the wording and tone of his will, which commences thus in the original Armenian:—

"Holiest Trinity and one Godhead, the Father, the Son and the Holy Ghost,—Preserve the undersigned Massy, son of Baba John, or otherwise known as Martyrose, who am an orthodox Christian by religion, an Armenian by birth, a native and citizen of Hamadan, a merchant by profession, and a resident of Calcutta under the Britannic Government. . . ."

He had brought his mother from his native town (Hamadan), and she had died and been buried at Calcutta before he made out his last will in 1794, in which he expresses a desire that, after his demise, his body should be interred in the Armenian churchyard of Calcutta, "next to my mother's grave."

Having no heirs, he left his fortune for the benefit of charitable and literary institutions. The clause, with reference to his property, reads:—

"I hereby divide my whole estate into sixteen equal parts and shares; eight parts of which I bequeath and give for the improvements of the Armenian city of New Nakhe Jevan* in the district of Azof, for the following

* New Nakhe Jevan, a town of European Russia, under the Government of Ekaterinoslav, is situated on the right bank of the river Don, two miles east of Rostov-on-the-Don. It has a population of 17,000, mostly Armenians, and was founded by the Armenian Archbishop of Russia,

institutions of that place, *viz.*, two parts for the national schools, two parts for the orphanage, two parts for the hospital, and the remaining two parts for the benefit of the alms-house,—all which shall remain there in everlasting memory of me and for the remission of my sins and for the benefit of our nation; and out of the remaining eight parts, I bequeath six parts for the relief of civil prisoners in the Court of Requests' prison of Calcutta and the remaining two parts I bequeath for the relief of poor and itinerant Armenians who may from time to time come to Calcutta from Armenia in search of their livelihood. . . . ."

He ratifies the above arrangements and terms in a subsequent clause, *viz.*:—

"My executors shall faithfully and honestly collect all the income accruing from my estate, and of the gross income they shall deduct their annual commission at the rate of five per cent. in December of each and succeeding year, and shall dispose of the nett income in January of each year in the following manner:

"They shall remit eight parts of the nett income to the Trustees in charge of the charitable and literary institutions in the Armenian city of New Nakhe Jevan as aforesaid. They shall also distribute two parts of the nett income amongst poor Armenians from Armenia in the same month of January. And they shall dispose of the remaining six parts of the nett income by relieving Christian civil prisoners in the Court of Requests' prison, paying off the debts of as many as the income in question will suffice, and liberate them during *Passion week;* but should there be no Christian civil prisoners in

---

Joseph. of the princely house of Dolgorouky Argooteantz, in the reign of Catherine II., Empress of Russia. during the latter part of the eighteenth century. Soon after its foundation, an Armenian priest, a Rev. Stephen, was deputed by the founder to India to collect donations from the Armenians of this country in aid of that newly-formed Armenian colony. The mission was a success, and it was through the tact of this Armenian priest that the testator was pleased to leave such handsome bequests in aid of the charitable and literary institutions of that place.

jail at any time, or they be few in number, and the amount exceeds the demand, then I desire and enjoin that with the surplus or the whole amount, as the case may be, they shall pay off the debts and relieve Mahomedan and heathen [Hindu] civil prisoners, for *such* shall be my *heirs* after my demise."

The large estate which he left, consisting of landed property and Government securities, is in the hands of the Administrator-General of Bengal, who, in terms of his will, remits annually to the trustees of the literary and charitable institutions of the Armenian city of New Nakhe Jevan their allotted portion; about Rs. 1,300 every year to the Calcutta Armenian Church Relief Fund, for the benefit of poor and itinerant Armenians from Armenia only; and after the payment of certain charges for the relief of prison debtors, the surplus, amounting to over Rs. 4,000 per annum, goes to the District Charitable Society, Calcutta, by order of the High Court.

In 1861, the Armenian community of New Nakhe Jevan erected a memorial over his grave* in the Armenian churchyard, Calcutta, through their representative, Michael Nalbandeantz, who was an able Armenian writer of merit. At the same time, he realised, on their behalf, all the accumulated income from the estate of Massy

---

* The inscription on the marble slab is to the following effect:—

"Sacred to the memory of the late respected patriotic Armenian, MASSY BABA JOHN, or, as he was otherwise called, ABDEL MASSY MARTYROSE. He bequeathed large legacies in his last will and testament for the intellectual culture of Armenian youths, for the relief of orphans and those imprisoned for debts, as well as for the support of distressed itinerant Armenians. This memorial is erected by the Armenian community of New Nakhe Jevan, in token of their everlasting thankfulness and gratitude.

"'Here let me rest, on Thee depend,
My God, my hope, my all.
Be Thou my everlasting friend,
And I can never fall.'

"Died in Calcutta."

Baba John, amounting to about Rs. 80,000, which was used to further their literary and charitable institutions, in accordance with the terms of the will, the provisions of which, as far as the above institutions were concerned, had up till then been disregarded by the executors. Another omission, an unpardonable one, was that they did not place a tombstone over Massy Baba John's grave, so that the exact date of his death is uncertain; in all probability it occurred in 1802, for the following reason:—In a valuable list, arranged chronologically from the year 1786 to 1820, which comprises all the donations given at various times by opulent Armenians for the benefit of the Calcutta Armenian Church and the poor attached thereto, I find the abovementioned sum of Rs. 1,300, the amount of the annual income allotted for the relief of poor and itinerant Armenians from Armenia from his estate, first mentioned under date of the year 1803. It may therefore fairly be assumed that Massy Baba John died in the previous year.

CHAPTER X.

HOW LOYALTY WAS REWARDED IN PROSPERITY AND ADVERSITY.

AGAH CATCHICK ARRAKIEL, an eminent merchant of Calcutta, already referred to at page 104, was succeeded by his eldest son, Agah Moses. Having inherited the loyalty of his esteemed father, he rendered valuable services to the British Government by raising in Calcutta, in 1801, and keeping up at his own expense, a company* of 100 Armenians, over whom he was appointed commandant, when the greater part of the army was required for active service in the Deccan against the French. For this act of loyalty, the Governor-General, the Marquis of Wellesley, was pleased to present him with a sword in a full *levée* at Government House.

In the now rare *East Indian Chronologist*, published at Calcutta in 1801 by a Mr. Hawksworth, there is a letter written by Agah Moses to him, which comprises a sum-

---

* An earlier instance of Armenian loyalty to the British cause in India is to be found in the now rare *Asiatic Annual Register* for 1799, in a proclamation issued on the 31st October 1798 :—

"Whereas the security and defence of this Presidency require that the Corps of Militia, composed of the inhabitants of the town of Calcutta, should be re-established and embodied under such regulations as the Right Honourable the Governor General in Council shall order and direct: His Lordship in Council, relying on the loyalty and public spirit of the inhabitants of the town of Calcutta, hereby orders and directs all the European, Armenian, and Portugueze inhabitants of the said town to assemble on the walk between Chandpaul Gaut and Fort William, to be there duly mustered and enrolled. The Europeans to assemble at the aforesaid place on Wednesday the 7th, the Armenians on Thursday the 8th, and the Portugueze on Friday the 9th of November, at day-break; and the proper officers are hereby commanded to attend, for the purpose of mustering and enrolling such persons as shall appear, and tender their services, according to the tenor of this proclamation."

The same *Register* has the following :—

"*Militia Orders, Fort William, December 21, 1798.*—The Governor General has observed, with the utmost satisfaction, the zeal and alacrity with which all ranks of the European, Armenian, and Portugueze inhabitants of the town of Calcutta have applied themselves to learn the use of arms, since the re-establishment of the Corps of European Militia," &c.

mary of the history of the Armenian colony at Calcutta. It reads:—

"Sir,—I have the pleasure to give you such an account of the Armenian inhabitants of Calcutta as I can confidently assert to be exact. I myself was born in that metropolis, and what I am about to write is the collective information from the oldest Armenians now living there. The Armenians settled in this country upwards of 150 years ago, and I feel a pride in adding they have been always faithful subjects to the English Government; by referring to Bolts you will find that my great-great-grandfather, Phanoos Calender [Khalanthar], was, in consequence of his confidential services to the English, honoured with several privileges and public rights from Government.

"Shortly after the establishment of Calcutta by the English, the Armenians settled among them and erected a small chapel in the China Bazaar, where Mr. Joseph Emin's house now stands. The site of the present Armenian church was at that time their burying-ground, in which there are tombstones dated 80 years back, and consequently older than the present church. The Armenian church was built in the year 1724 by one Aga Nazar, and the steeple was added in 1734 by one Manuel Hazarmall, the expenses attending which were defrayed with a sum appropriated for that purpose by his father, Hazarmall Satoor. The architect, Gavond, was an Armenian from Persia. No material alteration was made at the Armenian church from the above period until the year 1790, when my deceased father, Catchick Arrakiel, embellished the church inside, presented the clock, added the houses for the clergy, and built the surrounding walls. The church now goes by the name of St. Nazareth's Church, in honour of the founder. The church at Chinsura is the oldest that the Armenians have in this country. It was erected in 1695, and dedicated to St. John." *

---

* The Armenian Church at Syedabad was erected in 1758 and dedicated to the 'Holy Virgin Mary.'

For some time Agah Moses carried on successfully the business left him by his father, but suffered heavy financial losses during the war between England and France, when his two ships were captured by French privateers in the Indian Seas. He was greatly reduced in circumstances in his old age, when he was "too far advanced in life to enter on uncertain or hazardous undertakings." In 1833, we find him bringing his distressed circumstances to the notice and consideration of the Governor-General, Lord William Bentinck, with a view to obtaining employment under Government, to whom in his better days he had rendered devoted and yeoman service. The correspondence which passed between him and the Government is interesting from many points of view: it is therefore given *in extenso*:—

"*To the* RIGHT HONOURABLE LORD W. C. BENTINCK, G.C.B. *and* G.C.L.H., *Governor-General, and Council.*

"My Lord,

"Your Lordship having pleased to open the public service to all classes of Indian British Subjects, and His British Majesty's Ministers having manifested their intention to act on the same just and benevolent principles, I beg leave to offer myself to your Lordship's notice and to solicit such favourable consideration as the particulars of my case shall in your Lordship's judgment render me worthy. Your Lordship must be too well acquainted with the History of British India to need being informed that the British East India Company in first forming a settlement in this part of India received great assistance from my countrymen and especially from one Caja Phanoos Calandar. The high estimation in which the said services were regarded by the British Rulers of those days is abundantly recorded in Historical works and other Public Documents and it in part appears from the agreement between the Governor of the East India Company and members of our nation dated the

22nd June 1688 and from two other documents dated on the same day, one being a personal favour granted to the said Caja Phanoos Calandar. The titles of the said three Documents are given below* and a copy of the whole annexed severally marked A, B, C.

"The said Caja Phanoos Calandar in rendering assistance to the English Merchants trading to India may be said to have been the most distinguished of all the Armenians residing in India, and I trust that branch of his family whereof I am a humble individual have not failed as occasions offered duly to manifest their attachment to the British nation. Accordingly in the year 1789, on the recovery of His Majesty King George the III. from a grievous indisposition being known in India, Aga Cachick Arakel (Caja Phanoos Calandar's grand-daughter's husband and my revered father), in expression of the lively gratification which he felt on the occasion, liberated all the prisoners confined for debt in the Calcutta Jail, which act it appears was viewed in so favourable a light by His Majesty and the British Government that a Miniature of the King attached to a gold chain was sent out from England to be conferred on the said Aga Cachick Arakel.

"When this mark of Royal approbation reached Calcutta, my worthy and much esteemed parent having ceased to exist, it was publicly conferred on me his eldest son at a Levee by the Most Noble Marquis Cornwallis, who as also the Most Noble Marquis Wellesly desired me always to appear at their Levees and Public entertainments decorated with the said signal mark of their Sovereign's favour, a favour which I am informed is seldom conferred on a British subject.

"In the year 1801, when the British nation was at war with France and the greater part of the army of

* "An agreement made between the Governor and Company of Merchants of London trading to the East Indies and the Armenian nation dated 22nd June 1688, marked A. Two Documents, each headed Governor and Company of Merchants of London trading to the East Indies, to all whom it may concern send greeting, dated as above, marked B and C."

this Presidency was required to act at a distance against Tippoo Sultan,* the local British Government considered it expedient to raise a Militia at Calcutta and accordingly the Christian Inhabitants in general were desired to enroll themselves on this occasion, I at the desire of

---

* This is clearly a chronological error, for the war against Tippoo Sultan was terminated by the capture of Seringapatam, on 4th May 1799. Tippoo Sultan's father was Hyder Ali, who from being the son of a Pathan soldier of fortune, became one of the greatest men of that age. He first appeared in the political arena in 1749, as a volunteer in the army of the Hindu rajah of Mysore. By his courage, address, and vast military resources, he distinguished himself in a number of daring exploits, and was raised by the rajah to the position of Commander-in-Chief. He subsequently deposed his indolent and imbecile master, and proclaimed himself Sultan of Mysore in 1759. He carried on war successfully against the formidable Mahratta Confederacy, the Nizam of the Deccan and the English, who had entered into an alliance to crush his power. In 1779 in concert with a French force, Hyder Ali commenced hostilities against the British on the Malabar Coast, and in the following year he invaded their possessions in the Carnatic at the head of a large army of 83,000 men, cut to pieces a strong detachment under Colonel Baillie at Pollilore, and well nigh threatened the annihilation of the English settlements in India. Hyder Ali Khan Bahadoor, the greatest soldier and the most consummate statesman of the age, died in his camp near Arcot on the 12th December 1782. He left his kingdom and military operations to his son, the well-known Tippoo Sultan, or Tippoo Saib, as he was otherwise called. Following the policy of his illustrious father, Tippoo engaged in several wars against the English, and their allies the Mahratta Confederacy and the Nizam of the Deccan. To expel the English from India and to demolish the Mahratta and other Hindu States in India, was the governing idea of his policy. With this object in view he sought the assistance and succour of the Grand Signior of Constantinople, Zemaun Shah of Afghanistan and the French Directorate of Paris. He accordingly deputed two ambassadors to the Government of the Isle of France (Mauritius), where they arrived in January 1798, with dispatches for the 'Colonial Assembly' of that place, and also for the 'Executive Directory' of France. The ambassadors of Tippoo proposed to the Government of the Isle of France to form an offensive and defensive alliance against the British in India. The local Government duly sent the overtures of Tippoo to France and, being unable to supply any regular troops, forthwith issued a public proclamation in the islands of Mauritius and Bourbon, inviting volunteers to enlist in the Mysore Army. That proclamation contained, amongst others, the following proposition made by Tippoo: "That he [Tippoo] only waited for the succour of France to declare war against the English, and that it was his ardent desire to expel the English from India." The invitation was to a small extent responded to, and about 200 volunteers embarked with the ambassadors, who arrived at Mangalore on the 26th April 1798, and were duly admitted into the service of Tippoo Sultan. Napoleon Bonaparte was

His Lordship the Governor-General raised one hundred of my countrymen, and such of them as were not in affluent circumstances I clothed and occasionally armed at my own expense. I was appointed Capt. Commandant of this company and continued to command it as long as the Calcutta Militia was required by Government, also while holding this command the Governor-General the Most Noble Marquis Wellesly was pleased in a full Levee to confer on me with his own hands a sword to be worn whenever I was not on duty with my company, neither was this the only kind attention which I received from his Lordship. Thus favoured by my Sovereign and his representative in India I cheerfully bore the expense of clothing and occasionally arming my countrymen for the service of Government, nor did I repine when our connection with the British Nation

---

then in Egypt with his hitherto unconquered legions, dreaming of universal conquest. He wrote from Cairo an autograph letter to Tippoo in French, which can be rendered into English, thus:—

"FRENCH REPUBLIC.
"Liberty. Equality.

"*Bonaparte, Member of the National Convention, General-in-Chief,*
"*To the Most Magnificent Sultaun, our greatest Friend, Tippoo Saib.*

"Head-quarters at Cairo, 7th Pluviôse [26th January],
7th year of the Republic [1799], one and indivisible.

"You have already been informed of my arrival on the borders of the Red Sea, with an innumerable and invincible army, full of the desire of delivering you from the iron yoke of England. I eagerly embrace this opportunity of testifying to you the desire I have of being informed by you, by the way of Muscat and Mocha, as to your political situation. I would even wish you could send some intelligent person to Suez or Cairo, possessing your confidence, with whom I may confer. May the Almighty increase your power, and destroy your enemies. (Sd.) "BONAPARTE."

Tippoo's designs and his intrigues with the French were, however, prematurely disclosed, and war was declared against him, on his refusal to adhere to the new subsidiary system. A large British army was sent to Mysore from Madras and another from Bombay, with the addition of the subsidiary force of the Nizam of the Deccan. The war terminated with the siege and capture of Seringapatam by General Baird, and the death of Tippoo, who fell bravely fighting on the ramparts of his capital. His remains were deposited in the superb mausoleum of his father at Seringapatam with great pomp and solemnity. With him ended the short-lived dynasty founded by Hyder Ali in Mysore, which was, however, one of the greatest that sprung from the wreck of the Mogul Empire. His descendants have lived for nearly a century at Tollygunge, near Calcutta, as pensioners of the Government. Prince Muhammad Farrukh Shah, the present head of the Mysore family and one of the leading Muhammadan noblemen of Bengal, is the grandson of the late Prince Gholam Muhammad, one of the sons of Tippoo Sultan.

much more seriously affected my fortune and eventually produced my ruin.

"My father Aga Cachick Arakel was an eminent merchant in this Presidency. I was brought up and educated to carry on his business to which I succeeded on his demise. After having for some time successfully prosecuted my mercantile concerns in the late war between England and France, my two ships with much valuable cargo on board were captured by French Privateers in the Indian Seas. No Insurance could be effected in Calcutta. This serious misfortune together with heavy losses on my shipments to England obliged me to break up my commercial establishment in Calcutta. No longer able to carry on business entrusted from my father I engaged myself in manufacturing Indigo and many years industriously laboured in this my new vocation with various success. Eventually I might have succeeded but the late almost general failures of Calcutta agents depriving me in common with many others of the requisite pecuniary accommodation I was compelled to retire from my Factories and to make over to my agents.

"Thus when too far advanced in life to enter on uncertain or hazardous undertakings, I anxiously desire to obtain such employment under Government as will enable me creditably to support myself and family. Hoping I have ever acted as a faithful British Subject, also hoping I have never done any discredit to the reputation acquired by my revered Parent Aga Cachick Arakel and my ancestor the much esteemed Caja Phanoos Calandar, I respectfully solicit from your Lordship any such situation as I may be considered qualified to hold and I shall desire to enjoy public employment only so long as I faithfully perform the duties imposed on me.

"I am, my Lord, with the greatest respect,

"Your Lordship's

"Most Obedient Humble Servant,

(Sd.) "M. C. ARAKEL.

"Calcutta, 16th August 1833."

"General Department.

"*To the* HONOURABLE THE COURT OF DIRECTORS *for the affairs of the Honourable the United Company of Merchants of England trading to East India.*

"Honourable Sirs,

"We have the honour to submit for the consideration and orders of your Honourable Court the accompanying copy of a communication dated 16th of August last, from Mr. M. C. Arakel, an Armenian Gentleman, with copies of its enclosures.

"2. It appears that Mr. M. C. Arakel, who thus brings his altered and distressed circumstances to the notice of the Government, is the eldest son of Aga Cachick Arakel, an Armenian who displayed such generosity and benevolence at Calcutta in the year 1789 on the celebrations of rejoicings after the recovery of his Majesty George the III. by liberating all the debtors confined in the prison of the Court, which was considered by your Honourable Court so extraordinary an act of humanity and munificence that to testify your sense of such conduct your Honourable Court was pleased to forward a portrait of His Majesty to be presented to Aga Cachick Arakel, and having heard of his decease your Honourable Court directed in a despatch dated 16th of May 1792 that the portrait might be presented to his representative. This honour it would appear was conferred on Mr. M. C. Arakel, the present appellant.

"3. It would further seem that Mr. M. C. Arakel evinced his attachment to the British Government in the year 1801, at the time that a Militia was formed in Calcutta, on which occasion the Marquis of Wellesly presented him with a sword as a mark of his approbation and esteem.

"4. Mr. M. C. Arakel details the circumstances under which he has fallen into distress, and petitions the Government for relief by giving him some public employment.

"5. We have no employment in which we can make use of Mr. M. C. Arakel's services, and we do not feel ourselves competent to grant him a pension; but it is painful to associate his present straitened circumstances at an advanced period of life with the conduct which brought his father to the notice of the Honourable Court in 1789, and we therefore submit his case that your Honourable Court may if you think proper order some relief to be bestowed upon him.

"We have the honour, &c.,

(Sd.) "W. C. BENTINCK.

(„) "C. T. METCALFE.

"Fort William, 30th September 1833."

——:o:——

"General Department.

"*To* MR. M. C. ARAKEL.

"Sir,

"I am directed by the Right Honourable the Governor in Council to acknowledge the receipt of your letter dated the 16th of August last, applying for employment in some situation in the Public Service.

"In reply I am instructed to inform you that His Lordship in Council is much concerned to hear of the adversity of your Fortune, and proposes to bring your altered circumstances to the notice of the Honourable the Court of Directors, that they if they think proper may order the Government to make a provision for your declining years. I am directed to express the regret of His Lordship in Council that there is no situation at his disposal in the Public Service to which you are eligible.

"I am, Sir, Your most obedient Servant,

"G. A. BUSHBY,

"Offg. Secy. to the Government.

"Council Chamber, 30th September 1833."

——:o:——

"Barrackpore, November 27th, 1834.

"Dear Sir,

"I have the honour to inform you that the orders of the Honourable. the Court of Directors authorizing this Government to confer upon you such moderate pension for life as your situation and circumstances may appear justified by the Government upon public grounds. The subject, I am directed to add, will receive the attention of His Lordship in Council as soon as the weighty matters now pressing for decision are disposed of.

"I remain, Dear Sir,

"THOMAS PACKENHAM,

"Private Secretary."

——:o:——

"General Department.

"*To* MR. M. C. ARAKEL.

"Sir,

"With reference to your letter to the address of the Right Honourable the Governor-General in Council, under date the 16th August 1833, I am directed by the Right Honourable the Governor of Bengal to state that His Lordship has received the authority of the Honourable Court of Directors, to whom a reference was made on the subject as intimated in the letter of this Department to you dated the 30th September 1833, to assign a moderate stipend for life in aid of your reduced circumstances. An allowance of Sicca Rupees 100 per mensem has accordingly been made payable to your receipt from the General Treasury of this Presidency to commence from the 1st instant.

"I am, Sir, Your most obedient Servant,

(Sd.) "H. T. PRINSEP,

"Secretary to the Government.

"Council Chamber, 19th December 1834."

——:o:——

"*To the* RIGHT HONOURABLE GEORGE LORD AUCKLAND, G.C.B., *Governor-General of India in Council.*

"My Lord,

"When under the sanction of the Honourable the Court of Directors the allowance of a Hundred Rupees per month was given to me by Government, although understanding that His Lordship the Governor-General kindly wished to give a larger sum, I did not think it right then to solicit an increase because it was said that the Revenues of Government were not sufficient to meet the current expenditure here and in England; moreover, at the time in question I hoped that arrangements would be made respecting a large estate at Dacca which would prove beneficial to me, also other expectations existed, but I have been disappointed in all.

"During the intervening time I have been obliged to live on the allowance accorded to me, and it hardly can be requisite to state that even with the assistance of the extra 1,450 Rupees kindly given to me by His Lordship in Council, I have experienced very great difficulties in procuring the necessaries of life with the sum in question, and unless the Government please to augment my present allowance, my difficulties of course will increase. Now I understand that the Revenues of the country are more than sufficient to meet all demands both here and in England, I therefore presume that such increased allowance will be conferred on me as His Lordship the late Governor-General would have granted even under less favourable circumstances. His Lordship, before recommending my case to the consideration of the Court of Directors, satisfied himself through enquiries made to the Secretary Mr. Bushby that the representation contained in my address of August 16th, 1833, respecting the expenses incurred by me in the Calcutta Militia, was correct; but as that expense was incurred voluntarily, consequently I have no legal claim for remuneration. But as the amount expended by me in the service of Government (which amount Government would have paid) with accumulation of interest would at the present day procure for me a very considerable annuity, I hope therefore that this fact will be favourably considered on my applying for an increase of allowance. Being so reduced by my misfortunes as to need not only the comforts but it may be said even the common necessaries of life, I wished as long as Heaven blessed me with the ability to labour to have earned my bread by serving Government in such capacity as my humble services might be considered available, but His Lordship the Governor-General's kind consideration of my former condition in life caused him to decline offering me any situation which then could be held by any person not a covenanted servant of the Honourable Company. The correctness of what is here stated will appear from my address of August 1833 and upon Mr. Bushby's letter to me dated September 30th, 1833. I now most respectfully solicit that your Lordship will please to make such addition to my present allowance as will enable me to pass the few remaining years of my life with some degree of comfort.

"I am, my Lord, with the greatest deference,

"Your Lordship's Most Obedient Servant,

"M. C. ARAKEL.

"Calcutta, 30th October 1836."

Agah Moses Catchick Arrakiel died at Calcutta on 15th October 1843, aged 71 years. His remains and those of his brother, the Rev. Johanness, who was 52 years when he died on 20th October 1832, are buried inside the church, where inscribed marble slabs mark their tombs. Agah Moses had a son, whom he had called Catchick, after his deceased father's Christian name, but he died on 24th January 1812 at the early age of 21.

The late Agah Owen John Elias, who died at Calcutta in 1860, was another highly-respected member of the Armenian community of Calcutta and a wealthy zemindar of Bengal. He was born at Syedabad in 1786, and, though descended from a family of distinction, his outward bearing was meek and humble. His piety was without ostentation, and his charity knew no bounds; in the words of the poet, he "did good by stealth, and blushed to find it fame." Besides the inscription on the marble slab which covers his grave, two marble tablets—one in the Armenian church of St. Nazareth: the other, in the Medical College Hospital, Calcutta—testify to his genuine worth. The mural tablet inside the Armenian church has the following appropriate inscription:—

"Sacred to the memory of the late OWEN JOHN ELIAS, Esquire, born 1st November 1786, died 12th March 1860. This tablet is erected by the Armenian community of this place as a mark of their appreciation of his private and public virtues. His charities to widows and orphans and the poor will not remain unrewarded in heaven. His gifts to Churches, Schools, Asylums and Hospitals, which have made his name to be generally respected, have specially endeared it to his own countrymen."

Among the wealthy Armenian merchants of Calcutta in the present century, the name of Arratoon Apcar stands pre-eminent. He was the founder of the well-known firm of Apcar & Co., of this city. Born in 1779, at Julfa in Ispahan, he was the second son of Apcar, the ancestor of the family, unto whom were born six sons. At the age of sixteen he found his way to Bombay, where he entered the service of an Armenian merchant, with whom he found great favour. Being acquainted with the trade of China and Manilla, the energetic young man began with due circumspection to trade with those countries on his own account, after the merchant's demise. He settled and carried on his business for some time at Bombay * and afterwards removed to Calcutta in 1830.†

Apart from being an eminent merchant, Arratoon Apcar possessed all the virtues and characteristics of an exemplary Christian during his useful life. He was a true patriot and a philanthropist. Of a charitable dis-

---

* I have in my possession an autograph letter written by Arratoon Apcar from Bombay, and dated the 20th February 1815, to my great grandfather at Julfa, Ispahan.

† The diary of Mesrovb David Thaliatin, the Armenian poet, teacher and journalist of India, has the following, under date the 15th day of November 1830:—

"Sunday to be kept holy; but as it is the custom with our [Armenian] community in India to go visiting on Sundays, so I, after visiting several of my friends, went to pay my respects to Mr. Arratoon Apcar, who had *transferred* his business from Bombay to Calcutta.

position, he was ever ready to help the poor and needy. He was a true benefactor to those of his countrymen who were obliged, through adverse circumstances, to leave their homes in Julfa for India. His piety was of an exemplary character; he endowed the church of St. Mary, Julfa, where he had been christened, with munificent gifts, and also left it a handsome legacy, the annual income being remitted to the ministering priests attached to that church, for saying prayers for the repose of his soul during service on Holy Thursday night, when prayers are said over the graves of the departed. In 1843 he established the Armenian Patriotic School at Julfa, for the instruction of Armenian youths in their own and the Persian languages, which was more than now a desideratum, when there were no regular schools at Julfa. This school, which was maintained solely by Messrs. Apcar & Co., was a few years ago amalgamated with the Central National Academy of Julfa, to which institution that firm continue, as heretofore, to send their annual grant.

Arratoon Apcar died on 16th May 1863, aged 85 years. A marble tombstone, in the churchyard at Calcutta, bears the following inscription:—

"Sacred to the memory of ARRATOON APCAR, Esquire, the founder and up to the time of his death, for a period of 54 years, the senior member of the Firm of Apcar & Co., of Calcutta. Born at Julfa, in Ispahan, A.D. 1779; departed this life in Calcutta on the 16th May, A.D. 1863. Aged 85 years. '*Requiescat in pace.*'"

He had four sons, *viz.*, Apcar, Seth,* Thomas, and Alexander. The three former having departed this life, the present senior member of the firm of Apcar & Co. is Mr. Alexander Apcar. He is the respected head of

* Seth Apcar was the first Armenian Sheriff of Calcutta. He received from the Shah of Persia the Order of the Lion and the Sun (*Sheer-o-Khorshid*) through the Governor-General of India.

the Armenian community in Calcutta and is the Consul for Siam.

Gregory Apcar was a younger brother of Arratoon Apcar. He heard from his brother of his successful career, and came to India when quite a youth, in 1808, thirteen years after his brother's departure from home. He joined him while at Bombay, and was a member of the firm of Apcar & Co. until his death, in 1847, at the age of fifty-two. He was buried in the Armenian churchyard of Calcutta. On his marble tombstone the following lines are inscribed:—

> "Sacred to the memory of GREGORY APCAR, Esquire, an eminent Armenian merchant, highly and deservedly respected for his Christian and moral virtues. Born at Julfa, in Ispahan, A.D. 1795; and departed this life at Calcutta on the 23rd June, A.D. 1847. Aged 52 years."

He was succeeded by his son, Arratoon (Mr. A. G. Apcar), the present member of the firm, and the father of Mr. J. G. Apcar, now and for many years Clerk of the Crown.

The Apcars, one of the leading families of Calcutta, are the head of the Armenian community. Some members of that large family—descendants of the two brothers who founded the firm—have adopted the legal profession, in which more than one of them has distinguished himself by his eloquence.

CHAPTER XI.

ARMENIAN LITERARY INSTITUTIONS, ETC.

IT is a noteworthy fact that the Armenian colonists in India, amid their multifarious commercial pursuits, have neither been backward in the matter of education nor indifferent to the advancement of their national literature. This fact is evidenced by their efforts in establishing schools to train up and educate their children in the language and faith of their forefathers, without which their nationality could not have been so faithfully preserved in the land of their adoption.

One, named Margar, a *Commandant*,* used to instruct Armenian youths at his house in Calcutta; but the first regular Armenian school here was started in the year 1798 and conducted by Arratoon Kaloos, a native of Tokat† in Armenia. For twenty-five years he instructed Armenian youths in that language, and stimulated the Armenian community to further exertions in the cause

---

* In all probability this *Commandant* was the same "Margar Johanness Khalanthar of Julfa" (see p. 77) who served under Gorgin Khan in the Army he had raised and disciplined for the Nawab Meer Kasim Ali Khan.

† Tokat, the Armenian Evdokia, is a town of some importance in the *vilayet* of Sivas, a province of Armenia In the Armenian cemetery of that place may be seen the humble and sequestered grave of the Rev. Henry Martyn, B.D., chaplain to the Honourable East India Company and the pioneer of missionary enterprise in the East, who breathed his last at Tokat, on the 16th of October 1812, on his way to England from India *viâ* Persia. While in India, he translated into Hindustani the Parables and the New Testament; and he rendered during his prolonged stay at Shiraz, the far-famed seat of Persian literature, into Persian the Psalms of David and the New Testament.

of education. Among many others, the late Johanness Avdall received his education at the feet of this Gamaliel, whose memory he worshipped throughout his life, so much so that he had named one of his sons after his mentor, Arratoon Kaloos. The course of instruction at Arratoon Kaloos' school having been found insufficient for the progressive requirements of the period, the Armenian Philanthropic Academy was inaugurated, in 1821, at 358 Old China Bazaar Street, Calcutta, in the immediate vicinity of the Armenian Church of St. Nazareth.

The idea of a national academy was first conceived by one Astwasatoor Mooradkhan, who by his will, dated the 30th July 1797 (of which I have a copy in my possession), left sicca Rs. 8,000 towards the establishment of an Armenian school in Calcutta "for the education of the Armenian youth." To this nucleus were subsequently added further sums of money raised by subscription among the Armenian community through the strenuous exertions of the late Manatsakan Varden, who was greatly instrumental in collecting the subscriptions, as testified by the tablet erected to his memory.

The Armenian Philanthropic Academy was finally opened on the 2nd April 1821, and with it was amalgamated Arratoon Kaloos' school in 1825 at the express desire of the Armenian community. Arratoon Kaloos, who had devoted his life to the instruction of Armenian youth, died on the 11th November 1833, aged 56 years, and was buried in the churchyard of St. Nazareth, where his grave can be seen to this day. Being of a charitable disposition, he endowed the church of St. Nazareth with Rs. 10,000 for the relief of the poor attached thereto. A black marble slab was placed on the outside wall of the church to the west, with the following inscription:—

"In memoriam of ARRATOON KALOOS, Esquire, who endowed the church with ten thousand rupees for the relief of the poor."

In 1846 the members of the Armenian Philanthropic Academy paid tributes to the memory of the two patriotic founders of the institution by erecting within that institution two marble tablets. That to the memory of Astwasatoor Mooradkhan has the following:—

"Sacred to the memory of ASTWASATOOR MOORADKHAN, Esquire. This tablet is erected by the members of the Armenian Philanthropic Academy at Calcutta, to preserve the name and virtues of the abovementioned philanthropist, who, at his death, left a donation of eight thousand rupees by will, dated 30th July 1797, for aiding the establishment of such an institution. Died at Calcutta, 29th September 1799."

The other, to the memory of Manatsakan Varden, runs:—

"Sacred to the memory of MANATSAKAN VARDEN, Esquire. This tablet is erected by the members of the Armenian Philanthropic Academy at Calcutta, in acknowledgment of the high esteem and veneration in which he was held by their community, for his virtues in social life and zeal in behalf of the education and welfare of his countrymen, and in which he was at all times ready, equally with his purse and heart, and by his means, as well as the donations of other benevolent Armenians, *founded this Philanthropic Academy*, which dates its existence from the 2nd April 1821. Born at Julfa in Ispahan, on the 6th September 1772. Died at Syedabad in Moorshidabad, on the 14th October 1823."

With a view to preserve the names of those patriotic and opulent Armenians in India who have from time to time made handsome donations and left liberal bequests in aid of the Armenian Philanthropic Academy, the following list, which embraces a period of fully fifty years, from 1797 to 1850, has been carefully prepared:—

	Rs.	a.
Astwasatoor Mooradkhan	8,000	0
Manatsakan Varden	3,000	0
Yearly contribution of Rs. 1,560 from the Church of St. Nazareth, Calcutta, from 1820-1840 ...	32,760	0

	Rs.	a.
Elias Minas and Owenjohn Elias Minas, to 1848	38,920	0
Joseph Johanness Amirean	5,500	0
George Manook *	30,000	0
Malcom Manook	2,000	0
Stephen Mackertich	250	0
Aviet Agabeg	2,000	0
Martyrose Ter Stephen	1,000	0
P. Bagram and S. P. Bagram	2,000	0
George Phanoos Bagram	1,000	0
Sarkies Owen	500	0
Arratoon Petrus	1,000	0
Fatholah Hannah and Jubrah Usoff Asfars ...	1,000	0
Manuel Peter	100	0
Malcolm Gasper	100	0
Nazar Shahnazar	1,000	0
Johanness Hyrapiet	1,500	0
Thaddeus Satoor	1,000	0
Woskan Jacob	200	0
Adam George	20	0
Colonel Jacob Petrus of Gwalior	2,000	0
Simeon Gregory	200	0
Carapiet Arakiel of Penang	7,394	0
Agah Usoff Jevany	500	0
John Lucas	500	0
Hyrapiet Ter Gabriel	52	0
Aviet Philip Ptoom	100	0
Lazar Jacob	1,000	0
Sarkies Manook of Rangoon	1,000	0
Anthony Johanness Oozoom	200	0

* George Manook was the greatest Armenian merchant of Java in the early part of the nineteenth century. He enjoyed the friendship of the Viceroy of the island, and on several occasions lent large sums to the local Dutch Government. Born of poor parents at Julfa, Ispahan, he died a millionaire at Batavia on the 24th October 1827, aged 64 years. He lived and died a bachelor. In making out his last will and testament in 1820, he left the greater portion of his fortune of five million Dutch guilders to his two sisters at Batavia and the children of his brother, Malcom, who had died at Calcutta in 1826. The following liberal bequests, amounting to sicca Rs. 1,10,000, were left by him in aid of Armenian charities and literary institutions :—

	Sicca Rs.
The Armenian Philanthropic Academy of Calcutta	30,000
The Armenian School of Madras	30,000
The Holy See of Etchmiatzin in Armenia	25,000
The Armenian Monastery of St. James at Jerusalem	10,000
The Cathedral of All Saviour at Julfa in Ispahan	10,000
The Nunnery of St. Catherine at Julfa in Ispahan	5,000

	Rs.	a.
Catchatoor Galustaun * and Nierses Ter Mackertich of Penang	208	0
Arratoon Anthony	10	0
Johanness Simon	228	0
Kirakose Arratoon	400	0
Seth and Gregory Sam of Madras...	300	0
Carapiet Jacob	300	0
Pogose Jordan	300	0
Lazar Agabeg	374	0
Arratoon Kaloos	150	0
Manook Nicholas	500	0
Juntloom Aviet	2,000	0
The members' subscription in 1825	5,791	0
Carapiet Johanness Petrus	200	0
Thorose Gregory	1,000	0
Catchick Astwasatoor George	250	0
Rev. Joseph Stephen	250	0
Sarkies J. Sarkies	500	0
Arratoon M. David	500	0
Philip Astwasatoor George	100	0
Malchus Isaac Malchus	200	0
Vertanness Zachariah	50	0
David Barsick	100	0
Aviet J. Aviet	50	0
Gregory Astwasatoor Peter	16	0
Carapiet Arratoon Vertanness	125	0
George Gregory, surnamed Bonaparte	3,917	14
Reginald Heber, Bishop of Calcutta	100	0
The Armenian Community of Calcutta in 1828 ...	783	0
Contribution in aid of Orphan's education ...	1,000	0
Contribution from the Armenian Community of Singapore	500	0
Arratoon Apcar	1,000	0
Vardon M. Vardon & Bros....	250	0
Mesrovb David Thaliatin	25	0
J. G. Lucas' bequest	1,666	0

* Catchatoor Galustaun, or, as he was otherwise called, Agah Catchatoor, was a prominent Armenian merchant of Penang. There, in 1822, he erected the Armenian Church of St. Gregory the Illuminator at a cost of over $20,000. He died while on a visit to Calcutta in 1841, and on his tombstone, in St. Nazareth's churchyard, the following lines are inscribed :—

"Sacred to the memory of CACHATOOR GALUSTAUN, Esq., an Armenian gentleman, who for upwards of thirty years, was an eminent and respectable merchant in the Prince of Wales Island [Penang], where he erected a magnificent Armenian church entirely out of his own means: whose piety was without ostentation, and whose heart burned with true patriotism; whose happiness consisted in alleviating the wants of his distressed and itinerant countrymen; the charities and gifts of whose right hand were unknown to his left; who departed this transitory life at the age of 60 years on 26th January 1841 at Calcutta."

	Rs.	a.
Gregory Mooradkhan	20	0
Philip Catchick's bequest	2,625	0
Peter J. Sarkies	250	0
Mackertich S. Owen	250	0
Martyrose S. Owen	250	0
Johanness Avdall	200	0
Gregory Apcar	60	0
Manook M. Manook	250	0
Peter J. Paul	600	0
Joseph Agabeg	250	0
Johanness Agabeg	250	0
Aviet Galustaun	250	0
Apcar A. Apcar	250	0
Zorab M. Manook	250	0
Gasper M. Gasper	250	0
Johanness G. Bagram	250	0
Mrs. Hossanna M. S. Shookoor's bequest ...	1,000	0
„ Mariamjan Sarkies' bequest	5,000	0
„ Hripsimah Eleazar Lumbroog*	10,500	0

The Academy, during its existence of about three quarters of a century, since its foundation in 1821, has afforded shelter and education to many hundreds of Armenian youths from Julfa, Ispahan, and elsewhere. At present it is situated at 39 Free School Street and still continues its useful work.

Johanness Avdall, who was connected with it about forty years, first as a teacher and afterwards as a rector, was a native of Shiraz in Persia—the birthplace of the two famous Persian poets, Saadi and Hafez,—and the last resting-place of that immortal Armenian poet, Mesrovb David Thaliatin, whose name I bear. Johanness

* Mrs. Lumbroog, or Limburggen, also left a liberal bequest of over Rs. 40 000 to the Armenian church of Calcutta in aid of the poor. Her liberality was not, however, confined to Calcutta : she was resident at Madras, and contributed liberally to the Armenian church and charities of that place. A mural marble tablet, placed to her memory inside the Armenian church of St. Nazareth, Calcutta, has the following inscription :—

"Sacred to the memory of Mrs. Hripsimah Limburggen, who departed this life at Negapatam on the 21st May A.D. 1833. She was born at Surat in the year 1778. This tablet is erected as a mark of gratitude for her munificent bequest towards the relief of poor Armenians in Calcutta."

Avdall came to India when quite a youth, early in the present century. Being of a studious and retiring disposition, and having an insatiable thirst for knowledge, he devoted his days and nights to the study of Armenian and English, and soon distinguished himself as a scholar. For nearly fifty years he was connected with the Asiatic Society of Bengal, and had the honour of being the only Armenian member of that Society since its foundation in 1784. In 1827 he dedicated his first literary work, an English translation of Dr. Chamich's *History of Armenia*, to the president and members of that learned Society. He translated into Armenian Johnson's *Rasselas* and some other works of English authors.* His literary fame was surpassed, however, by that of his contemporary, the late Mesrovb David Thaliatin, already referred to, whose standard works bear ample testimony to his literary attainments.

There was a Girls' Department in the Armenian Philanthropic Academy when it was founded: it was abandoned in 1842. The late Mesrovb David Thaliatin, amid his multifarious literary pursuits, started in 1846 the Armenian Infant Seminary, which he dedicated to the tutelar Saint, Sanduct—an Armenian princess who suffered martyrdom for her Christian faith in the forty-eighth year of the Christian era. This self-supporting school had a boys' as well as a girls' department, where Armenian and English were taught by a staff, superior to that of the Armenian Philanthropic Academy and inferior to no English schools existing in Calcutta in those days. The *Englishman*, in its issue of the 21st January 1850, made the following remarks:—

* Johanness Avdall died on the 11th July 1870, aged 67 years, and was buried in the Armenian churchyard of St. Nazareth, Calcutta.

"THE ARMENIAN INFANT SEMINARY (*dedicated to their tutelar Saint, Sanduct*).—The fourth annual examination of this little seminary, of not only boys, but of little girls, took place at the premises near the Armenian church on the 14th instant; and was actually attended by a larger assemblage of respectable ladies and gentlemen than was anticipated. The Armenian history, grammar, &c., was examined by the clergy of that nation, assisted by some lay gentlemen, and the English by the Revs. Messrs. Thompson and Sinclair. Both the boys and the girls acquitted themselves commendably. Their translations from English into Armenian have already appeared in the Armenian newspaper published at the same premises. Specimens of Armenian and English handwriting, arithmetic, as well as ornamental needlework and knittings were laid on the table. Even children of the indigent are taught here, although no donation or bequest is hitherto made to this little institution. After the examination, a short address was made, prizes awarded, and a merited benediction followed by the vicar of the Armenian church. At the close of it, an appropriate hymn was chanted by the children in their own language. As the Philanthropic Academy does not educate *girls*, had this little seminary not been projected by Mr. Mesrop David Taliatin, one of the previous students of the ever-to-be-lamented Bishop Heber's Scholarship (of blessed memory) at the Bishop's College here, assisted by his wife, and other Masters and Mistresses, the little girls of that nation would have remained neglected without their national education."

This seminary was closed after an existence of six years, having been insufficiently supported by the Armenian community, who were indifferent to the study of Armenian, and even pronounced it a *dead language.* It is noteworthy that, during its brief existence, many Armenians of both sexes, a few of whom are still living, received a sound education in Armenian and English.

at the feet of Thaliatin. To his efforts the revival of Armenian literature and nationalism in India is mainly due; for, through the medium of his journal, the *Patriot of Ararat*, he revived the dying embers of patriotism amongst the Armenians in this country.

Born in 1803, he was a native of Erivan in Armenia, and died at Shiraz in Persia in May 1858. A marble mural tablet, erected in the Armenian church of that city by his devoted friend, the late Thaddeus Catchick Avetoom of Calcutta, bears an inscription in Armenian metrical verse, of which the following is a translation:—

"Here in this dark tomb rests MESROVB DAVID THALIATIN, who was an erudite professor, a profound scholar, an eminent poet and historian. The entire society of Armenian *literati* shall always honour thee with enthusiasm, and neither New Julfa nor Calcutta forget thee for ever. Died 10th June 1858."

From his youth upwards he had an ardent desire for knowledge, and early distinguished himself as an Armenian scholar. He left his native country and came to India *viâ* Persia in 1823. Arriving at Calcutta he was soon admitted into Bishop's College as a foundationer by Bishop Heber, whose memory he reverenced throughout his life. The studious youth devoted his days and nights to the acquisition of knowledge, studying English, Latin, Greek and Persian, besides theology and the fine arts; these he mastered in five years, and, at the close of his successful scholastic career, the Board of Education certified him as a Master of Arts. His object in coming to India was to study the cultured languages of classical and modern times, with a view to impart to his countrymen the benefits of occidental education and learning. During the course of his studies at Bishop's College, he translated the learned treatise of Hugo Grotius, on the *Truth of the Christian Religion*, from Latin into classical Armenian. The Armenian translation of the treatise was submitted to the Publication Committee of that College, who unanimously decided to publish the work at their own press for the benefit of the Armenian nation.

Armenian type was cast, and the book was published in 1829, under the direct supervision of Thaliatin. He dedicated it to Messrs. Gregory and Seth Sam, two notable Armenian merchants of Madras. The Armenian community subscribed liberally to that now exceedingly rare publication, for which the late Colonel Jacob of Gwalior gave the handsome donation of Rs. 400. In 1830, he produced a metrical Armenian translation of *Palestine*, a prize poem by Bishop Heber, whose life he embodied in a biographical sketch that he published as a preface to the translation by way of a tribute to the memory of his patron, who departed this life at Trichinopoly in April 1826. Shortly after, he published at the same press his third publication in Armenian language on Mythology, which he dedicated to Sarkies Johanness Sarkies, an eminent Armenian merchant of Calcutta. Leaving Bishop's College in 1831, he directed his steps towards his native town in Armenia. After an eventful stay of about ten years in Armenia, Persia and Turkey, and having established several schools in various centres for the education of the Armenian youths, he returned to India in 1840, when he was welcomed at Bishop's College as an inmate, where he published in 1841 the *History of Ancient India* in the high-flown language of ancient Armenia. He dedicated the book to the late Arratoon Apcar, whose portrait formed the frontispiece. He was acquainted with many men of learning and distinguished oriental scholars in Calcutta, and had the good fortune to enjoy the friendship of the late Dr. R. O'Shaughnessy, M.D., Assistant Surgeon in the Bengal Army and Professor of Surgery and Medicine in the Medical College of Calcutta, to whom he dedicated in 1846 an Armenian work of great literary merit, *Annals of the Antiquities of Armenia*, "as a small token of esteem and gratitude by his most obliged servant, M. D. Thaliatin."

In 1845, through his strenuous exertions and with the hearty co-operation of the late Manook Zorab, Thaddeus Catchick Avetoom, and a few other Armenian gentlemen of Calcutta, the Araratean Society was formed for publishing books, &c., in the Armenian language. The Society had for its organ the *Patriot of Ararat*, an Armenian literary journal, ably edited and conducted by Mesrovb David Thaliatin. During the short space of two years (1845-1847), besides editing the journal, superintending the Press and the Seminary of St. Sanduct, that highly-gifted scholar published about ten original works, justly held in high repute, in the classical language of Armenia.

The Armenians, in 1820, founded an almshouse, commonly known as *Kheyrat Khanah*. At present it is situated in Pollock Street—the house being the gift of the late Agah Arratoon Petrus, the founder,—and is mainly used as a shelter by poor Armenian strangers to Calcutta. A black slab, with an Armenian inscription in verse, stands over the gate, of which the following is a translation:—

"This almshouse of the Armenian nation was erected by the munificence of the pious ARRATOON PETRUS, whose wife's name was AZIZ, and to whose memory he erects this to receive the strangers of our nation. He was zealous of the glorious deeds of his illustrious and hospitable ancestors. 1820 A.D."

In the *Calcutta Review* for July 1891, the Rev. Graham Sandberg observes:—

"Everywhere, it would seem, except in their native land, they are notably prosperous; the richest merchants and bankers in Eastern towns belonging to this nationality. Confirmed money-makers, they are lavishly charitable to their own people; and in a philanthropic investigation in Calcutta, concerning the distributing of charitable relief to the poor of all nations in that city, only one Armenian was reported to be in want—a man who had offended the community by leaving their Church."

CHAPTER XII.

THE ARMENIAN SETTLEMENT IN SOUTHERN INDIA.

IN Southern India the Armenians were equally successful in their commercial pursuits. They flourished at Madras during the seventeenth and eighteenth centuries, when they had the trade of the Carnatic in their hands, and carried on a lucrative trade with Europe and the East. From a valuable Armenian manuscript, written at Masulipatam by Sarkies Johanness in 1790, I find that the Armenians settled *permanently* at Madras in the year 1666. These opulent merchants were famous for their piety and true philanthropy, and for the great zeal they evinced in the advancement of Armenian classical literature in India. Their patriotism is perhaps unparalleled. They appealed to Catherine II. of Russia to free Armenia from the galling yoke of the Muhammadans and place it under her suzerainty. Two millionaires volunteered to place their millions at the disposal of the Russian Government for the purposes of the projected war, but, somehow or other, the project was not matured.

The *first* Armenian Church at Madras was erected as far back as 1712. It was one of the few magnificent edifices in the Esplanade of that city, but the Armenians were obliged to desert it after a time, as the British authorities would not permit so high an edifice to stand in the immediate vicinity of the Fort. The Latin Church in the same neighbourhood was objected to for the same reason, and demolished. The present Armenian

Church, situated in Armenian Street, was erected in 1772, and dedicated to the Holy Virgin Mary, the site being the old Armenian burying-ground, on which, moreover, a chapel stood, where they worshipped while the present church was in course of erection. The ground was the property of the famous Agah Shameer. His wife, Anna, had been buried there in 1765, and a room built to her memory. This room, which is still known as 'Shameer's Room,' was attached to the church that was built seven years afterwards.

The most eminent Armenian merchant at Madras in the earlier half of the eighteenth century was Khojah Petrus, son of Khojah Woskan, and a grandson of the famous Khojah Pogose of Julfa. He was a true philanthropist and an earnest patriot in helping and succouring his countrymen. He was strongly attached to the English, and was one of the members of the Hon'ble East India Company's Council of Madras. It is recorded that, on the occasion of the visit of the Nawab of Arcot to Madras, he received him with great *éclat*, entertained him for some days, and had all the principal streets through which he had to pass draped in silk. The Nawab, greatly appreciating the loyalty of the Armenian merchant, requested him to name a wish, which would be granted then and there. Khojah Petrus asked for the sole monopoly of the import trade to Madras and into the interior. This request was immediately granted. He thus amassed considerable riches, but sustained heavy losses in the troublous days when the French captured Madras in 1746 under Lally and totally demolished all the public buildings. Thirty-three houses belonging to him in the city were levelled with the ground, besides other houses that he had in the Fort.

The French, moreover, seized all that he had in the Fort and carried the spoil to Pondicherry. He took refuge in a Danish town close to Madras, and Count Lally sent him a message to place himself under the protection of the French Government, when the property confiscated by them would be restored. He spurned the overture, replying tersely and sarcastically that whatever riches he had possessed, had been acquired under the auspices of the British Government, to whom he would remain loyal, and that the French were at liberty to confiscate his goods, which would help to replenish their depleted treasury. In spite of these heavy financial losses, he left, in cash alone, at his death in 1751, the considerable sum of seven lakhs of rupees.

This notable merchant constructed, in 1725, a long bridge of many arches over the river Adyar, which flows through the hills* of St. Thomé (Thomas) and the village of Mamlan at the southern extremity of Madras. He is said to have spent over the bridge the sum of 30,000 hoons, *i.e.*, pagodas (each pagoda being equivalent to Rs. 3-8), and placed a large sum in the British treasury, the annual interest accruing thereon to meet the necessary repairs. There is another hill, about six miles from Madras, the supposed site of the martyrdom of St. Thomas, the apostle of India. A Christian church has long been in existence at its summit, and is frequently visited by the devout. In 1726 Khojah Petrus caused 160 broad stone steps to be made at his own expense from the foot to the top of the hill, with spacious resting-places at intervals.

* There is a church on one of these hills, now in the hands of the Latin clergy, where many tombstones exist to the present day bearing Armenian inscriptions, dating early in the seventeenth century, from which I infer that the church was erected by the Armenians during that period.

A life-size oil painting, executed at Madras in 1737, of this highly patriotic Armenian gentleman, is to be seen at All Saviour's Cathedral at Julfa in Ispahan. The noble and pious Khojah is represented in old-style Armenian garb. With a pen he writes in Armenian, 'The fear of the Lord is the beginning of wisdom.' On one side of the painting is the figure of a heart neatly painted, and beneath it a metrical verse in Armenian, composed by Khojah Petrus himself, the following being a translation:—

"My heart longs for home, where, should I be unable to go, I desire that, when my last day comes, my heart be sent to my native town, so that I, PETRUS WOSKAN, shall have a grave there."

These lines bear strong testimony to his patriotism, which knew no bounds, so much so that he desired that his heart should be taken to the land of his birth for interment. It is a popularly-accepted tradition in Julfa that his heart was brought after his death from Madras enclosed in a golden box and buried there (at Julfa), in accordance with his wishes.

This was not the first instance, however, of an Armenian sojourner in India having expressed a fervent desire to be buried at his birthplace after his demise, as will be seen from the following circumstance. Up to a very recent date there was to be seen a solitary tombstone in the ruins of the palatial houses and villas on the banks of the Zenderood river in the city of Julfa, erected by the opulent Armenian merchants of bygone days. The tombstone bore an inscription in the Armenian language, which may thus be rendered into English:—

"Jesus Christ, Lord of all, when Thou sittest on the Judgment seat of the Great Tribunal, have Thou mercy on AGAH MAROOTH, on his father THASALY, on his mother KHANPHASHY, on SUGMEER his wife, and on SIMON his son *who died in India*, and whose body was brought from thence and buried in this spot in the year 1706 A.D.

May God have mercy on his soul, on his brother APOVEN, and on his sisters AGAHY and GUNGUN."

Khojah Petrus made out his last will and testament in 1750, bequeathing large sums for various places of pilgrimage for Christians, as well as for the establishing of charitable and literary institutions at Julfa, where he was born. He died at Madras in 1751, prior to the erection of the present Armenian church, and his remains were interred in the churchyard of Vepery of that city. His tombstone, bearing an inscription in Latin, reads:—

"Elata fama in auras, interque nubila caput condens, hic ingressus solo jacet. Discordium conciliator, jurgiorum placator, Armeniorum fautor, columenque firmum, indigentium præsidium, fervidumque tutamen, impendiosus, largusque refector, in Divina, ædesque sacras propagando haud perparcè strenuus impensè,—PETRUS USCAN DE COJA POGUS, Armenius, cujus cor Julfæ; Annos natus 70; e vita decessit, 15 Januarii 1751."

It may be translated thus:—

"Here [at Madras] lies buried one whose fame extended far and wide, even to the heavens; an advocate of peace, an intercessor in disputes, a patron and unfailing stay of Armenians; a helper, zealous protector, and liberal, open-handed benefactor of the poor; one by no means sparing, but generously active, in supporting the Church and in the dissemination of Divine Truth,—PETRUS USCAN DE COJA POGUS, an Armenian, whose heart is [interred] at Julfa; aged 70 years; departed this life on the 15th January 1751."

Another Armenian merchant who rose to eminence in Madras was Agah Shameer Soolthanoomean. He was born at Julfa in 1723. Coming to India in early life, he settled at Madras, where he flourished during the latter part of the eighteenth century. He was a famous pearl merchant and also carried on a lucrative trade in Persian rose-water and dried fruits imported from his native town. By selling them at immense profit to the Nawab of the Carnatic and to his luxurious household, he amassed considerable riches. He lent large sums to the Nawab of the Carnatic, and the debt was not cleared off when the English took his country. It is recorded that, when the Nawab was being oppressed by his many creditors, Agah Shameer went to pay his respects, and had the Nawab's promissory note with him. The Nawab asked, "And do *you*, my dearest friend, entertain any fear as to my financial position, and have therefore come to demand your just claims from me?" The noble Agah Shameer replied: "Not so, my lord. I have come as usual to pay my humble respects to Your Highness. My claim against you is but a little dust from your shoes!" And as he spoke he took out the Nawab's promissory note from his breast pocket, tore it up, and threw the pieces at the Nawab's feet. This magnanimous act, which appears little short of a romance, excited the enthusiastic admiration of the Nawab and his courtiers, and the grateful debtor ordered the title-deeds of the village of Noomblee to be brought to him. He then ordered his Private Secretary to write out a *firman*, which he duly signed and sealed, to the effect that he was pleased, of his own free will, to grant the village of Noomblee, with all the lands attached thereto, to his valued and esteemed friend Agah Shameer, as a personal gift, who would be its lawful owner, and could do whatever he liked with the same. Neither his heirs, nor the British Government, were in any way to annul the provisions contained in the deed of gift which was bestowed on Agah Shameer, and he was exempted from paying any taxes thereon. The village of Noomblee was to remain the property of Agah Shameer and his descendants for ever. This large property was owned by the Shameer family of Madras until of late years.

This Armenian millionaire, when at the zenith of his glory, sent valuable presents to the Emperor and

Empress of Russia. In return the august Emperor conferred upon him the little city of Loree, in the suburbs of Tiflis, as a mark of his appreciation, and also invited the esteemed Agah Shameer to settle there with his children.

There existed at Madras at one time a life-size portrait of this distinguished personage, dressed in Armenian costume and national head-gear, with the following articles arranged before him:—A pair of scissors, a yard measure, a pair of scales with small weights for weighing precious stones, and an ink-pot with a quill pen; in his hand is a row of large pearls which he is offering to a jeweller for sale. This was adopted as the crest of the Shameer family, and it is carved on all the tombstones of the Shameers who lie buried at the Armenian churchyard of Madras. Agah Shameer, the head of the family, died at Madras * in 1797, and an Armenian inscription, of which the following is a translation, appears on his tomb:—

> "Here lies interred the body of the noble SHAMEER SOOLTHANOOMEAN, an Armenian, who was born at New Julfa on the 4th November 1723, and died here at Madras, on Saturday, the 13th day of June 1797, aged 74 years."

He left three sons, *viz.*, Jacob, Johanness, and Eleazar. Jacob was born at Madras in 1745, and died at *Malacca* in 1774 in the prime of life. He had inherited his father's patriotism. This is clearly illustrated from the pathetic epitaph on his tombstone at *Malacca*.† Naturally studious, he was enthusiastic in the advancement of classical Armenian literature in India. To him is due the honour of having started at Madras in 1772 the *first* Armenian press in India, of which more hereafter. Johanness was born at Madras in 1757, and died a poor man in 1834, leaving only one daughter. He is buried in the Arme-

* A road in Madras bears Shameer's name.

† See page 30, footnote.

nian churchyard of Madras. Eleazar was likewise born at Madras, in 1758, and, like his eldest brother, died at the age of 29, in 1787. He was buried in the Armenian churchyard of Madras.

Agah Samuel Moorad, whose noble heart glowed with patriotism, was another Armenian merchant of great wealth at Madras. His name will be handed down to posterity for his benevolence and zeal in the cause of educating indigent Armenian youth and orphans. He left a large bequest for the establishing of a school in Europe for Armenian youth, which should be under the control of the Mekhitharist Fathers* at

* This is a religious band of erudite Armenian monks, leading a monastic life, who are styled 'Adopted Sons of the Virgin, Doctors of Penitence.' For their arms they have a Cross surrounded by the four emblems of St. Anthony *viz.*, the Flame, the Bell, the Gospel, and the Staff. The Society is called after its founder, Mekhithar, an Armenian monk from Sebastia (the modern Sivas), whose memory is dear to all lovers of the classical language of ancient Armenia. Endowed with gifts of a high order, Mekhithar saw the deplorable state of neglect into which Armenian literature had sunk owing to the political troubles of Armenia, and conceived the happy idea of founding a monastic order having for its object the advancement of classical Armenian literature and the intellectual welfare of the Armenian nation. After travelling through Armenia and Asia Minor, the missionary priest arrived in 1700 at Constantinople, a great Armenian centre, where he endeavoured to found his project. At Pera, a pleasant suburb of Constantinople, Mekhithar, with three of his disciples, started a printing-press and published a few religious and educational works in the Armenian language. His efforts in that direction were frustrated, however, through the machinations of the ignorant clergy of that time, and he had to flee from Constantinople. After encountering many hardships, he and his disciples found a refuge at Modon, a town in Morea, then under the government of the powerful Venetian Republic. For twelve years he remained undisturbed at Modon, and was then obliged to fly before the Turkish invasion of Morea, who took Modon and pillaged and burned the monastery which Mekhithar had established at that place. Thanks to the kindness of the humane Venetian Admiral and the Governor of Morea, they not only sympathised with the destitute monks, but granted them permission to embark in a government vessel bound for Venice. On their arrival there, in April 1715, the twelve hapless Armenian monks were hospitably received by the Republic. The Senate, regarding with favour the great project Mekhithar had in view, was pleased to confer upon him and his followers for ever the Isle of St. Lazarus (San Lazzaro) in the vicinity of Venice, on which there had once been a Leper Asylum. Mekhithar, with his

Venice. They deputed to Madras one of their *confrères*, the Rev. Dr. Sarkies Theodorean, to realise the endowment; and, after a protracted law-suit in the Madras Court, Rs. 640,500 were paid to him on 26th March 1827 by Edward and Johanness, Agah Samuel Moorad's sons and executors.

In 1834, the Mekhitharist Fathers first opened a College in the name of the founder at Padua in Italy; in 1846 it was changed to Paris; and subsequently removed to Venice, where, through the bounty of Edward Rafael, another rich Armenian of Madras, a similar institution had been opened in 1836, and named Rafael College, after its patriotic founder. Under the supervision of the Mekhitharists, both these institutions continue their useful work in educating Armenian youth in the vernacular and the modern European languages. Some of the former students of these Rafael and Moorad

small hand of devoted followers occupied the island, where he erected an Armenian monastery, which was completed in 1740, with a church, school, printing-press and all the accessories of a monastic institution. In that abode of peace, the pious Mekhitharist monks have devoted their lives to study and research. They have rendered valuable services to the literary world in general and the Armenian nation in particular. They have edited and published the Armenian classics and have also rendered into classical Armenian the works of the classical writers of ancient Rome and Greece, for the benefit of the Armenian nation. They have from time to time published many original works of great literary merit on the history, literature, antiquities and archæology of Armenia. Classical Armenian literature might have sunk into inevitable oblivion, but for the lifelong devotion of the zealous and erudite Mekhitharist Fathers at Venice and Vienna, to whom the entire Armenian nation owes a deep debt of gratitude. Byron, who studied Armenian with the Mekhitharist Fathers, wrote from Venice on 2nd January 1817:—

"On my arrival at Venice in the year 1816, I found my mind in a state which required study, and study of a nature which should leave little scope for the imagination, and furnish some difficulty in the pursuit. At this period I was struck—in common, I believe, with every other traveller—with the Society of the Convent of St. Lazarus, which appears to unite all the advantages of the monastic institution without any of its vices. The neatness, the comfort, the gentleness, the unaffected devotion, the accomplishments, and the virtues of the brethren of the order, are well fitted to strike the man of the world with the conviction that there is another and a better even in this life. These men are the priesthood of an oppressed and a noble nation," &c.

Colleges hold appointments in the Military and Civil Services of Persia and Turkey, and many other Armenians in humbler positions owe their success to the bounty of these patriots of this country in the early half of this century.

The following extracts are interesting and of historical value. Under date the 29th February 1779, a Rev. Johanness Ter Nierses wrote to the Armenian Archbishop of Julfa a long letter from Madras, in which, after giving full particulars of the war between the French and the English, he said :—

" At present commerce is at a standstill, and French ships are scouring the seas and capture every vessel that comes in their way. A Danish ship bound for Batavia from this city of Madras was seized by the French, whereby our [Armenian] merchants sustained a heavy loss."

The same clergyman, writing from Madras on 15th January 1784, observed :—

" It is three years now that we are in the midst of a serious war. There was a great scarcity of eatables, and great difficulty was experienced in procuring food, and whatever could be procured was very expensive, owing to which more than half of the population of this city perished through famine, but at the commencement of the war our [Armenian] community were divided into three parts—one part went and settled at Negapatam and Seringapatam, one part settled at Masulipatam, and one part remained at Madras."

From this it will be seen that the increasing Armenian colony of Madras formed three parties about the year 1781. One section settled at Negapatam and Seringapatam; another remained back at Madras; and the third settled at Masulipatam, where they erected a church. A few Armenian families remained at Masulipatam down to the middle of the present century.

CHAPTER XIII.

AN OLLA PODRIDA OF INTERESTING EVENTS.

IN the early part of the eighteenth century, the Armenians settled and formed a colony at Dacca, when it was one of the commercial centres in Bengal. There they flourished in commercial pursuits for a considerable time, and amassed great riches, for they had the trade of the place in their hands, and also held considerable lands and zemindaries. Originally they had built a small chapel, where they worshipped prior to the erection of the present church. Five miles from Dacca is the old Armenian cemetery at Tejgaon, where many a tombstone with Armenian inscriptions can be seen. The oldest is to the memory of one Avetis, an Armenian merchant, who had died at Dacca on 15th August 1714.

In 1781, the present Armenian church of the Holy Resurrection at Dacca was erected by subscriptions from Michael Sarkies, Astwasatoor Gavork (George), Khojah Petrus, and Margar Pogose, in the locality known to the present day as *Armanitola* (Armenian Street), and the belfry was afterwards added by the late Sarkies Johanness Sarkies. The ground was the gift of Agah Catchick Minas, and on it stood the small chapel already referred to, for there are tombstones in that churchyard which bear inscriptions dating back to 1762, or about twenty years earlier than the erection of the present church on the site of the old chapel. The following pathetic epitaph, in Armenian metrical verse, is from a tombstone there :—

> "Oh, you gazers at poor me, see the hopes of this vain world, what it promises and what it does, and where it sinks at last, as in the case of poor me. My name is JOSEPH, and I am the son of CATCHICK. On the completion of my twenty-eighth year, my life is taken by sad death and, instead of going to my native town, which is known in the classics as Thupgees [Tiflis], I was buried here under this sepulchre, and my body was placed in the bosom of mother earth on the 8th day of Damah [5th November] 1811 A.D."

In the early part of the present century the most eminent Armenian merchant and zemindar of Dacca was the famous Agah Arratoon Michael, who died a millionaire in 1824. The founder of the Dacca Pogose School, Mr. Nicholas Pogose, was another rich Armenian zemindar of Dacca. That once-flourishing colony is reduced to a few families only, as in the case of Madras and Bombay.

About the middle of the eighteenth century, the Armenians formed a commercial colony at Bombay. Their name will always be associated with the locality known as Armenian Lane, in the vicinity of the Armenian church, where the opulent Armenians resided in the good old days. Here they flourished for a considerable time as traders, but eventually dwindled away, only a few families now being left.

In 1796, through the munificence of Jacob Petrus, an opulent Armenian merchant of Bombay and a native of Hamadan in Persia, the indispensable national church was erected for divine worship in the Fort, a locality which has always been of great commercial importance owing to its favourable situation and the proximity to the harbour. It is situated at 45 Medows Street, where an Armenian priest is maintained for the spiritual requirements of the few Armenian families and of the native Christians who have embraced the Christian faith in the Armenian apostolic church. At the foot of the altar of the church is a square tablet with an inscription in Armenian, of which the following is a *verbatim* translation:—

> "This holy church was erected in the name of the holy Apostle Peter, during the Patriarchate of His Holiness Lucas, the Catholicus of all the Armenians, by the munificence of Mr. JACOB of Hamadan, to the memory of his late parents, Mr. PETRUS, his father, and ZANAZAN KHATOON, his mother, the foundation-stone of which was laid by Archbishop James, who was on an evangelical tour in India on behalf of the Holy See of Etchmiatzin in the year of our Lord 1796, on the 14th day of Thirah [12th October]."

Another tablet, over the door of the sacristy, bears the following inscription, here translated from the original Armenian:—

> "The outside parts of this holy church with the buildings attached thereto were repaired by the munificence of AGAH JACOB, son of ARRATOON THAGEANTZ, to the memory of his late mother, the noble lady THAMAR, and his sister [Miss] ANNA, dead in Christ. The repairs were executed through the instrumentality of Archbishop James, on the 3rd day of Shams [4th April], in the year of our Lord 1801."

The inscriptions in the Bombay churchyard do not go beyond the present century, but there are five tombstones, bearing Armenian inscriptions, in the compound of a private dwelling-house at 9 Victoria Road, Byculla, a suburb of Bombay, the earliest being for 1767. The occupant of the house permitted me, this year, to make exact copies on the spot of the inscriptions, which were composed in Armenian verse, in accordance with the time-honoured custom. The monolith tombstones of fine granite are all in a row in a separate enclosure, with a small door attached, and are fairly well preserved. These tombs are adjacent to an old building still standing, built in the original style, where the solitary Agazar family resided in the eighteenth century, when there was no Armenian church or cemetery at Bombay. They were therefore obliged to bury their dead without any ceremony in their own compound, and their bones have since lain there undisturbed.

Let us now turn to the troublous times of the Indian Mutiny* of 1857-58, and see how some Armenians were thereby affected. We have already seen that Major Owen Jacob was murdered and mutilated by the fanatical mutineers at Agra, while commanding the troops of the loyal Maharajah Scindia of Gwalior against the rebels. At Lucknow, where the Mutiny broke out with much fury, another Armenian, a respectable merchant, sustained heavy financial losses through the outbreak, which shook the British rule in India to its foundations. In March 1892, I visited that historical city, the capital of the once-powerful Nawab-Viziers of Oudh† from 1775 to 1856. I visited the Residency, which has been immortalised by the poet‡ and the historian, and whose sad, interesting ruins bear silent, but eloquent, witness of the past. My guide, an English gentleman, had been one of the brave juvenile defenders of the 'Martinière Post,' which was composed of the masters and boys of La Martinière College of that city, named after Claude

---

* By a strange coincidence the Indian Mutiny broke out exactly a hundred years after the famous victory of the British Army under Clive at Plassey on the 23rd June 1757, which laid the foundation of the British Empire in India.

† On the annexation of Oudh by the British in 1856, the last of these —Wajid Ali Shah—was deposed and deported to Calcutta, where he lived and died a State prisoner at his palatial residence in Garden Reach on the 21st September 1887, in his sixty-eighth year. By the ex-King's death the dynasty founded in 1732 by Saadat Khan, the Persian merchant of Nishapur, became extinct.

‡ Tennyson, in his heart-stirring ode on 'The Defence of Lucknow,' pathetically describes the prolonged siege and the glorious defence of the Residency, which is without parallel in Indian history.

Martine,* its founder. The various interesting spots within the sacred precincts of the Residency were indicated by him. No visitor can help being affected by the touching epitaphs and laconic inscriptions in memory of those gallant soldiers of the beleaguered garrison who fell while upholding England's prestige. With a feeling of awe and veneration I looked upon the crumbling walls of the Residency buildings which had been battered by the shot and shell of the rebels. Who cannot but admire the patriotism of those who heroically defended the place against innumerable odds, for a hundred and forty-seven days, before the arrival of the Relief party under Generals Outram and Havelock?

---

* Of obscure French parentage and from being a Private in the French Army, Claude Martine rose to the rank of Major-General in the Hon'ble East India Company's service. Through his endowments, his name will be handed down to posterity as an eminent philanthropist. He was born at Lyons on 5th January 1735 and, after receiving a good mathematical education at a public school, he entered the army at the age of twenty, and landed in India as a common soldier with a French armament under the famous Count de Lally in the eventful year 1757. In January 1761 he was taken a prisoner-of-war by the English at Pondicherry and sent to Bengal, where, after the conclusion of the war, he joined the service of the East India Company. Being strong in mathematics and engineering, he was deputed in 1773 to make a survey of the province of Oudh; and at the request of its ruler, the Nawab-Vizier Sujah-ud-dowlah, he was permitted to attach himself to the Court of Oudh Sujah-ud-dowlah, with whom Martine had found great favour, died at Fyzabad, the former capital, on 26th January 1775, and was succeeded by his son Asaf-ud-dowlah, who removed the seat of government to Lucknow. Martine remained in the service of this enlightened prince, whose reign was favourable to foreign art and enterprise. At Lucknow he opened a bank and started other profitable commercial undertakings. A cannon foundry was soon in full swing; not only that, but he made gunpowder, coined rupees, built houses, planted parks, and introduced amongst native lapidaries the Dutch system of cutting diamonds, and succeeded in building up an immense fortune. Besides large landed properties in India and France, he left more than four millions of sicca rupees invested in the Company's Paper, at that time Twelve Per Cents. After providing for his dependants, and bequeathing £25,000 to his relations at Lyons, and a similar sum to the Lyons Municipality for its poor, he left the greater part of his fortune for the purpose of founding colleges at Lyons, Calcutta, and Lucknow, each to be called after him. He left a large bequest for establishing an *industrial* school at

Being an Armenian, I was much interested in a square pillar outside the Residency grounds, to which a marble slab was affixed, bearing the simple inscription, 'Johannes House.' My guide informed me that Johannes, who was a well-known Armenian merchant of Lucknow, seeing the dark clouds rising in the horizon of Indian politics, betook himself with his wife and child into the Residency. The building, the site of which the pillar marked, was double storied. There Johannes resided and conducted his business. It overlooked the Residency buildings, and the rebels took possession of it, and from its lofty terrace kept up an incessant fire into the compound of the Residency. Ultimately the house was blown up by those besieged, as it was too dangerous a rendezvous for the enemy, "who swarmed in Johannes' house." Besides

---

Lyons, of which I have no data. He bequeathed sicca Rs 3 50,000 for the La Martinière Institution at Calcutta, which was opened on the 1st March 1836 and has since held a prominent place as an educational establishment. Out of his estate, the sum of sicca Rs. 8 16,444 was decreed by the High Court of Judicature, Calcutta, for the support of the college at Lucknow, which was inaugurated in 1840 at the Constantia Mansion of the founder. In his will he thus refers to his favourite mansion:—"My Constantia House is never to be sold. It is to serve as a monument, or tomb, to deposit my body in, and the house is to serve as a college for educating children and men in the English language and religion." This imposing edifice, one of the architectural ornaments of Lucknow, was designed and built by Claude Martine as a residence for himself during the reign of Asaf-ud dowlah, who offered Rs. 1,00,000 for it on its completion, but was refused. It is in the Italian style of architecture and highly ornamental. The General's motto, '*Labore et Constantia*,' is inscribed in prominent characters on the front of the building. At the La Martinière, Lucknow, which in 1869 was affiliated with the University of Calcutta, one hundred foundationers are fed, clothed and educated free of charge General Martine died, on 13th September 1800 at the Farhat Baksh Palace, also built by him as a residence and his remains were enclosed in a vaulted chamber in the basement of the Constantia House, where his tomb—a simple sarcophagus—stands on the floor, bearing the following literal inscription, which was composed by himself and inserted as a stipulation in his will:—

"Major-General CLAUDE MARTINE, born at Lyons, January 1735, arrived in India as a common soldier, and died at Lucknow, on 13th September 1800, and he is buried in this tomb. Pray for soul!"

Johannes, his wife and child, there was another Armenian, one Carapiet Arathoon, a juvenile defender of the 'La Martinière Post,' who lost his life in the garrison.

A fair idea of the extent of the trade carried on by the Armenian merchants of Julfa with India and the Far East may be gathered from the following valuable and carefully-prepared list of those Indian towns with which the Armenian merchants of Persia were acquainted and held commercial intercourse in the seventeenth century. This list was prepared in the Armenian language by one Costand, an Armenian schoolmaster at Julfa, at a time when the enterprising Armenian merchants of the commercial city of Julfa were commercially at the zenith of their glory and ventured into the remotest parts of Asia in their commercial pursuits :—

"Cashmere, Peshawar, Mooltan, Attock, Sirhind, Janabad [Shahjehanabad, *i.e.*, Delhi], Akbarabad [Agra], Khurja, Hundwan(?), Bangalah [Bengal], Behar, Phathanah [Patna], Benares, Moven [? Mawāna], Ghazipore, Jalalpur, Shahzadpur, Khairabad, Daryabad, Daulatabad, Sirhinj [? Sironj], Berhampore, Surat, Gujerat, Aurungabad, Shahgarh, Hyderabad, Moochleebandar [Masulipatam], and Bhutan."

From India Costand passes on to "Pegu, Ava [Mandalay], Khata(?), Cotta, Cochin, Chirbad(?), Senan(?), Malacca, Batavia, Ternate, Amboyna, Macassar, Timor, Solor, Manilla, and Sharnov(?)." Among Eastern towns, Kabul,* Kandahar, Ghaznee, Balkh, Bokhara, and Meshed are mentioned in the list.

* The Armenian traders, who penetrated as far as Manilla in the Far East, also formed a colony at Kabul, situated on the old caravan route to India from Persia and the East. Afghanistan is regarded politically as the 'Buffer State,' and Kabul its capital has always been a commercial centre of considerable importance. At one time it contained a flourishing Armenian colony, consisting of thirty well-to-do families, who, as colonists, built

The pupils attending Costand's school were the sons of wealthy Armenian merchants, who, trading extensively with foreign countries, paid special attention to the education of their children. They were instructed by Costand in the vernacular and the rudiments of commercial knowledge. Among the many precepts which Costand desired to impress on their minds, were:—

"Do not start on a journey alone. Do not sit and sleep with one whom you have not known and tried; perhaps he may murder you on the way and plunder you of all your goods. Take provisions from your own pantry and a companion from your own house. Keep the paper for writing in your breast [pocket], pen and ink in your coat pocket; the lamp in your luggage; the scales with the weights in its box; the yard measure

---

themselves a national church. Kabul, not unlike the many Indian cities where the Armenians had settled and erected churches, was included in the extensive diocese of the Armenian Archbishopric of Julfa, the jurisdiction of which extends from the north of Persia to the Far East, including India and the East Indies. The Archdiocese of Julfa, as far back as the thirties, sent priests to Kabul, and the Armenian colonists there, despite their reduced circumstances, managed to maintain the priest sent to them. For some years afterwards they were left without a priest, as the diocesan bishops of Julfa neglected their little fold in far-off Kabul, where the Armenian colonists had for ages tenaciously preserved their nationalism and the faith of their forefathers, isolated as they were in a Muhammadan country. They were therefore obliged to bury their dead without any religious ceremony. Their offspring were left unbaptised until the memorable year 1839, when the Indian Government, under Lord Auckland, the Governor-General, sent an expedition to Afghanistan for political reasons, to place the Durrani Shah Shuja upon the throne of Kabul in the place of Dost Mahammad Barakzai, the usurper. The army escorting the exile Shah Shuja from Ludhiana made its way through the Bolan Pass to the Afghan capital, and Shah Shuja, in August 1839, was led triumphantly into the historical *Bala Hissar* at Kabul and enthroned. Dost Mahammad soon after surrendered to the British, and was sent to Calcutta as a State prisoner. On the entry of the British troops into Kabul, the Armenian residents went in a body to the military chaplain with the forces. At their entreaties he accompanied them to their national church, where divine service had not been held for some years. There they brought forward their unbaptised children, whom he baptised in accordance with the rites of the Anglican Church. The Armenians of Kabul, in their priestless state, stood faithful for a time to their national religion, but Amir Shere Ali forced them to embrace Muhammadanism, and converted their church into a mosque.

[iron] in your belt; your senses in your head; and your mind towards God. Be satisfied with what God may give you. Do not trust an unknown person with a parcel. Record all your daily transactions; and do not put off till to-morrow what you can do to-day."

Costand died at Julfa in the year 1702 A.D., and was buried in that part of the cemetery which is allotted to the Armenian monks. A tombstone, bearing a terse inscription in Armenian, the following being a translation, marks his grave:—

"This is the tomb of COSTAND, the scholar, who led a monastic life and died in Christ in 1702 A.D."

Many of the towns enumerated in Costand's list have long since been forsaken by Armenians; but up to the middle of the present century they were to be found in the following towns in India and the Far East, as a pontifical bull from the Holy See of Etchmiatzin, dated 31st December 1850, is addressed to the Armenian residents at "Calcutta, Chinsurah, Syedabad, Dacca, Agra, Gwalior, Cawnpore, Lucknow, Fattihabad, Lahore, Bombay, Surat, Hyderabad, Madras, Masulipatam, Rangoon, Moulmein, Ava [Mandalay], Penang, Singapore, Malacca, Batavia, Semarang, Sourbaya, Thegal, Jeparah," &c.

It is difficult, indeed, to conjecture what India might to-day have been if, coupled with their enterprise and perseverance, the Armenians had adopted an aggressive policy in India.

CHAPTER XIV.

PROMULGATION OF ARMENIAN LITERATURE IN INDIA.

THE Armenian colonists evinced a keen interest in the advancement of classical Armenian literature in India down to the middle of the present century, and were greatly instrumental in starting printing-presses in those Indian towns where the Armenian element was strong. Accordingly, Armenian printing-presses were started at Madras, Calcutta, and Bombay towards the end of the past century.

The first Armenian publication in India, printed at Madras, dates back to the year 1772. The interesting title-page may thus be literally rendered into English:—

> "New pamphlet, called *Exhortation*, composed for the awaking of the Armenian youth from the weak and idle drowsiness of the sleep of slothfulness, and with an ardent and tender desire printed at the expense and through the exertions of Jacob Shameer by his tutor Moses Bagram, for the benefit of the tender Armenian youth, in the year of the incarnation of the Word 1772. and in the year 1221 of the Armenian era. In India, at the city of Madras, at the press of the same Jacob Shameer."

The works in the Armenian language, published at Madras between the years 1772-1800, possess considerable literary merit.

It is a curious fact that the *first* Armenian journal ever printed in any part of the world was published at Madras, a hundred years ago, by the Rev. Arratoon Shumavon, an Armenian priest of Shiraz, whose name is dear to all interested in the study of classical Armenian. He started the *Azdarar* (*i.e.*, 'Intelligencer') on

28th October 1794, and published it monthly for eighteen consecutive months until February 1796. Its centenary jubilee was celebrated, however, in 1894 by Armenian journalists in Constantinople, Smyrna, Tiflis, Venice, Vienna, Marseilles, and America; and, in commemoration of the event, the religious society of the Armenian *literati* (the Mekhitharists) at Vienna, of the monastic order of the great Mekhithar,* published an artistic phototype of the venerable father of Armenian journalism.†

While at Shiraz, the Rev. Arratoon Shumavon had the misfortune to lose his two sons in one week. Overcome by grief, he left his fold and retired from the city. He took up his abode with the Persian *dervishes* (anchorites) in the solitude of Babakoh, 'far from the madding crowd.' This hill (the Parnassus of the Persians) being within easy distance, however, of the city, was the favourite haunt of the two famous Persian poets, Saadi and Hafez, who frequently resorted thither to invoke their muse. The Armenian cemetery of Shiraz nestles at the foot of this hill, and there sleeps the immortal poet, Mesrovb David Thaliatin.

For seven long years the bereaved Shumavon remained with the Persian *dervishes* at Babakoh, and studied closely the flowery Persian language—the French of the East,—which he completely mastered, and distinguished himself as a Persian scholar. Yielding eventually to the entreaties of those who were dear and near to him, he returned once more to the city from which he had

---

* See page 148, footnote.

† In connection with this jubilee, the Rev. Dr. Gregoris Galemkharean, a member of the well-known Mekhitharist Society of Armenian monks at Vienna, published in 1893 an opportune work—the first volume of the *History of Armenian Journalism* from 1794-1860—and dedicated it to 'The Armenian journalists of the day.'

turned his face. Shortly afterwards he departed from Shiraz, with its melancholy associations, and came to Madras—which at that time contained an influential Armenian community solely engaged in commerce—as a minister for the Armenian church of that place. The patriotic Armenians of Madras had already shown a praiseworthy zeal for the advancement of classical Armenian literature, and they warmly seconded his endeavours in that direction. About 1789 he started a printing-press at Madras for printing and publishing books in the Armenian language. In the absence of any trained workmen, he acted as compositor and printer. Not only that, but the type used was cast by himself from materials prepared by his own hands—a large undertaking, even in the present day, which few would attempt single-handed. The first publication from his press, in 1789-90, was a reprint of *The Martyrology of the Virgin Marianeh.* The interesting title-page may be rendered into English thus:—

"An account of the Holy Virgin Marianeh. reprinted from a copy originally printed at Constantinople in the year 1766 A.D., and now printed in India, at this capital of Madras, from type prepared by the Rev. Arratoon, son of Shumavon of Shiraz, for the benefit of the Armenian youths, in the year of our Lord 1789."

The indefatigable printer adds an interesting notice at the end of the book, dated 30th January 1790, from which it appears that only two hundred copies of it were printed at the expense and through the exertions of the Rev. Arratoon Shumavon, "by the grace of God a priest of Shiraz," in honour of his intimate friend, the noble Agah Marooth Joseph, of the family of Phurnacheantz.

The *Azdarar*, referred to already, gave an impetus to the study of the Armenian language in India amongst the Armenian colonists. At its start it had the modest number of *twenty-eight* subscribers, and the first number was issued on the 30th of Thirah (28th October) 1794, "during the patriarchate of His Holiness Lucas, the Catholicus of all the Armenians at Valarshapat, and in the reign of His august Majesty, Heraclius II.,* King of Tiflis, under the protection of the [Armenian] church of the Holy Virgin at Madras, at the press of Rev. Arratoon Shumavon of Shiraz." Among its contributors was the well-known Archbishop Joseph, of the princely house of Dolgorouky Argootheantz, the founder of the Armenian city of New Nakhe Jevan in Russia during the reign of Catherine II.† Besides literary articles and contributions, it contained the principal events of the time. Announcements of births, marriages, and deaths amongst the Armenian community of Madras, commercial and shipping intelligence, and the advertisements of the Armenian merchants of Madras, are

* Heraclius II. was a Georgian prince educated in the camp of Nadir Shah, King of Persia. He accompanied him on his memorable expedition to India in 1739. In 1733 Georgia had fallen under the sway of Nadir Shah, that obscure soldier of fortune from Khorassan, who had, in 1730, delivered Persia from the Afghans, driven out the Turk, and, at the unanimous request of the principal nobles and officers of Persia, ascended the throne on the morning of the 26th February 1735. After Nadir Shah's tragic death in 1747, Heraclius restored the kingdom of Georgia and was proclaimed King at Tiflis. To ensure the safety of his country against his neighbours, who were constantly at war with him, Heraclius declared himself in 1783 a vassal of Russia, but was abandoned by the Russians in 1795, when the Persians, under Agha Muhammad Khan, invaded Georgia, defeated Heraclius, captured and destroyed Tiflis the capital, and led a great number of its inhabitants into captivity. Heraclius II. died in 1798, and was succeeded by his son, George XIII., a weak-minded prince, whose short reign was throughout disturbed by a civil war against his brothers. After his death, in 1800. Georgia was annexed by Russia, and the members of the royal family were carried to the Russian capital. Alexander, another son of Heraclius II., took refuge in Persia; but his wife—the daughter of Melik Sahak (Isaac), an Armenian nobleman of Erivan in Armenia—was taken to St. Petersburg with her son. Alexander ended his days in exile, dying in poverty at Teheran, and lies buried there in the Armenian churchyard.

† See page 110, footnote.

to be found in its pages, and even 'answers to correspondents' were not neglected. Through his profound knowledge of the Persian language, he found great favour in the eyes of Valaji Mahamad Ali Khan, the Nawab of Madras and Arcot, from whom he received permission in 1795 to print and publish books in the Arabic and Persian languages as well. A copy of the Nawab's *firman*, granting him permission, was duly lithographed in fine Persian and Arabic characters and published in the *Azdarar* (pp. 253, 254) of that year.

Following the example of Madras, in 1797 an Armenian press was started at Calcutta through the exertions of another Armenian priest, the Rev. Joseph Stephen, incumbent of the Armenian church of St. Nazareth, Calcutta. The first publication issued from it was a valuable account of a controversy on the Truths of the Christian Religion, which took place between an Armenian monk of Julfa, named Johanness,* deep in theological lore, and the crafty monarch, Shah Safee, otherwise known as Shah Sulaiman I.,† who, it may be

* Johanness, a saint and scholar, had, through his profound knowledge of theology, as well as the Persian and Arabic languages, won for himself the honourable title of 'The Theologian of Kings.' He was the author of several theological works in Armenian of great merit, and left a few valuable works—original and translated—in Persian and Arabic, on theology and the Christian religion.

† Sulaiman Shah ascended the throne of Persia in 1665. He was the eldest son of Shah Abbas II., and the grandson of Shah Abbas the Great, who has been referred to on page 26. After an uneventful reign of twenty-nine years, spent in debauchery, Sulaiman Shah died in 1694 at Ispahan, the former capital of Persia. He was succeeded by his son, the bigoted Shah Sultan Husain; and during the troublous reign of this indolent king, the Afghans invaded Persia in 1722, and laid siege to Ispahan, and, by preventing supplies reaching the besieged, starved it into surrender. The proud Persian king, humiliated at last, with his own hands placed his crown on the head of Mahmud Ghilzai, the Afghan king, and wished him prosperity. Mahmud ascended the throne of Persia, and the Sefavi dynasty, founded by Ismail I. in 1502, was practically at an end. The Afghan rule in Persia lasted for eight years only, from 1722-30, when Nadir Shah drove the Afghans from that country.

mentioned, was desirous of converting the Armenians at Julfa to Muhammadanism, but failed in his scheme. According to the printer's preface. it was printed from a manuscript, dated 15th December 1724. I possess a copy of this now exceedingly rare publication, printed in the same year (1797) by the zealous Rev. Joseph Stephen "at the newly-started press under the protection of the Armenian church of St. Nazareth, Calcutta." It was published "at the sole expense of the illustrious Agah Moses, son of the late Agah Catchick Arrakiel of the Juntloom family of Julfa." The MS., with its pages alternately in Armenian and Persian, remained in the possession of the printer, the Rev. Joseph Stephen, who afterwards presented it, with another valuable MS. in Armenian by the same writer, to the library of Bishop's College, Calcutta.

In 1811, another press was started at Calcutta by Aviet Juntloom. An elementary book, in the Armenian language, was the first publication issued from it. This press was presented, on 1st January 1824, to the Armenian Philanthropic Academy, by the same Aviet Juntloom, and less than two decades since it was at work. The second Armenian journal started in India, styled the *Mirror*, was published at Calcutta in 1820. After a brief existence, its place was taken by the *Magazine*, which followed the same course. The *Patriot of Ararat*, already referred to on page 139, was the fourth Armenian journal in India. It was published at Calcutta, from 1845-52, under the able editorship of Mesrovb David Thaliatin, the Armenian poet, teacher and journalist of India. This highly instructive journal occupies an honourable place in the history of Armenian journalism.

CHAPTER XV.

CONCLUSION.

ABOUT the middle of the present century we find the Armenians in India adopting the legal profession. The present head of the Calcutta Bar, the Hon'ble Sir Gregory Charles Paul, K.C.I.E., the learned Advocate-General, who is also a member of the Bengal Legislative Council, is an Armenian. His father, Mr. Peter Jacob Paul, was a prominent member of the Armenian community of Calcutta, by whom he was highly and deservedly respected. He rendered valuable services to the Armenian Church, in his private capacity, as a legal adviser, up to his death in 1862. His talented son, the learned Advocate-General, was first educated at La Martinière College, Calcutta, where he won the gold medal; and, in 1846, he proceeded to England to complete his education. In due course he graduated at Cambridge, and was called to the bar. He returned to Calcutta in 1855, and commenced practising in what was then the Supreme Court, now known as the High Court. By dint of perseverance, and being gifted with abilities of a high order and commanding an easy flow of language, he rose to his present high position.

The following list, chronologically arranged, comprises the names of Armenian Advocates of the Calcutta High Court from 1855 to 1893:—

Inn.	Names.	Year of admission.	Appointment or Chambers.
L.	Hon'ble Sir Gregory Charles Paul, B.A., K.C.I.E.	1855 ...	*Advocate-General.*
I.	J. H. W. Arratoon, B.A.	1864 ..	England.
I.	Gasper Gregory (deceased) ...	1868 ...	Durbhungah.
I.	G. J. Pogose	1869 ...	Dacca.
I.	Aviet Agabeg	1869 ...	England.
I.	Thomas Alexander Apcar	1870 ...	11 Old Post Office St.
L.	Malcolm Peter Gasper* (deceased)	1872 ...	England.
L.	Arrakiel Peter Gasper	1872 ...	9 Old Post Office St.
L.	J. G. Apcar	1874 ...	*Clerk of the Crown.*
I.	John A. Apcar	1875 ...	High Court.
I.	A. Arathoon	1875 ...	England.
I.	A. A. Shircore	1875 ...	Chittagong.
I.	St John Stephen, B A., LL.B. ...	1880 ...	9 Hastings St.
I.	J. N. Pogose	1882 ...	Allahabad.
I.	A. E. Gasper	1882 ...	High Court
I.	A. T. Apcar, M.A., LL.B.	1883 ...	11 Old Post Office St.
M.	A. A Avetoom	1885 ...	11 Old Post Office St.
I.	Osmond J. Bagram	1887 ...	Rangoon.
M.	M. Zorab	1889 ...	6 Hastings St.
I.	Walter Gasper Gregory	1889 ...	5 Old Post Office St.
M.	John George Bagram	1890 ...	Bar Library.
I	G. I. M. Gregory	1890 ...	Mozufferpore.
I.	C. A. O. T. Gregory	1891 ...	High Court.
G.I.	J. Ernest Bagram	1893 ...	Bar Library.
M.	John Chater Jordan	1893 ...	N.-W. P.

* The late M. P. Gasper was one of the leaders of the Calcutta bar. He was a respected member of the Armenian community of Calcutta, and they paid a tribute to his memory, by erecting a marble mural tablet in the Armenian church of St. Nazareth, which bears the following inscription:—

"Sacred to the memory of MALCOLM PETER GASPER, Esq. (barrister-at-law), eldest son of Peter Malcolm and Madeline Gasper; born at Calcutta 15th June 1848, died at sea off Aden, 3rd August 1890, aged 42 years 1 month and 19 days; who, after taking the medal at the Doveton College, Calcutta, in the year 1863, completed his education in England, where he was the first Armenian student who appeared and successfully competed for the Indian Civil Service Examination in the year 1869; but, his health failing him, he soon after qualified for the bar and came out to India in the year 1872. By his own exertions he attained a prominent position among the leading members of the local bar, in which he distinguished himself by his exceptional talents. The untimely loss of one whose future was so bright and promising has been deeply mourned by a large circle of friends and admirers, who, being members of the Armenian community, have erected this tablet to his memory."

The only Armenian Pleader practising in the Appellate High Court is Mr. Chater Gregory, who was enrolled in June 1860.

There are also several Armenian Attorneys and Solicitors of the Calcutta High Court, as will be seen from the following list :—

J. R. Shircore	... ...	India 1856	... Allahabad.
Martin Camell	... ...	India 1866	... Also Notary Public.
L J. Arathoon	... ...	India 1870	... Umballa and Simla.
Galstaun Gregory	...	India 1870	... Firm of Gregory and Jones, Solicitors.
Elijah Owen Moses*	...	India 1870	... Also Notary Public and Pleader of the Appellate High Court.
John Camell	... ...	India 1875.	
J. A. Apcar	... ...	India 1889.	
O. Camell	... ...	India 1891	... Solicitor.

Besides these, a few Armenian Pleaders practise in the Police and Small Cause Courts of Calcutta and elsewhere in India.

The Medical Profession, too, has allured Armenians during the second half of the present century.

The late Dr. J. M. Joseph of Madras, who rose to the rank of Deputy Surgeon-General, was the first Armenian who joined the Indian Medical Service as far back as 1852. After a useful career he retired on the 1st July 1885, but did not live long to enjoy his pension. The *Daily Post* of Bangalore had the following sketch of his career in its issue of 3rd July of that year :—

"Last Tuesday's *Fort St. George Gazette* notifies that Deputy Surgeon-General J. M. Joseph, M.D., has been permitted to retire from the public service from the 1st instant, on a well-earned pension of £950 per annum, supplemented by an annuity of £400, after having completed a very creditable career extending over well nigh

---

* Mr. E. O. Moses has been the President of the Armenian Association of Calcutta since its foundation in 1890.

thirty-three years of varied professional experiences and good honest work. Looking back on his past official life, the worthy doctor has good reason to be proud of his career; and the credit he has earned in the Department which he has served so well, as well as the general popularity he has secured outside the arena of his official duties, will lend additional lustre to the distinction he has so worthily attained.

"Dr. Joseph received his preliminary education under private tuition [at Bombay], and his entire medical training at St. George's Hospital, London, and in the St. George's School of Medicine adjoining that well-known institution. During the whole of his pupilage he was under the personal tuition of Dr. Samuel Armstrong Lane, the distinguished Anatomist and Surgeon of London, and the author of several scientific works. His earlier professional labours began at the Theatre of Anatomy attached to St. George's Hospital, where he for some time discharged the duties of a Demonstrator of Anatomy. In 1846 he obtained his diploma as a member of the Royal College of Surgeons, London, and six years later secured the degrees of Doctor of Medicine and Master of Surgery of the University of Glasgow. In 1858 he was elected a Fellow of the Royal College of Physicians of Edinburgh, and two years later became a Member of the Royal College of Physicians of London. The honorary degree of LL.D. was conferred upon him by his University in 1866, and in the same year he was, after a regular course of study, called to the Bar by the Honourable Society of the Inner Temple.

"His public career in connection with the Indian Medical Service began in November 1852, when he was nominated as an Assistant Surgeon on the Madras Establishment by Sir James Weir Hogg, the then Chairman of the E. I. Company's Board of Directors. Landing at Madras on the 1st of January 1853, Dr. Joseph was attached to the General Hospital there, but was soon after directed to do duty with the left wing of H. M.'s 94th Regiment, then stationed at the Bangalore

Fort. Hundreds of his former patients here and elsewhere will bear grateful testimony to the fact that his genial manners and thorough-going character, no less than his professional skill, have earned for him a very large share of popularity and lasting esteem from every class of society with which he was come into contact during his long, active, and eminently useful public career."

The grades of his official career were as follow:—Assistant Surgeon, 20th November 1852; Surgeon, 14th December 1864; Surgeon-Major, 20th November 1872; Brigade-Surgeon, 27th November 1870; Deputy Surgeon-General, temporary rank, 25th April 1879; and Deputy Surgeon-General, permanent rank, 16th May 1880.

Descended from an old Armenian family of Surat, Dr. Joseph was born at Bombay* on 16th April 1826, and died at Madras in his sixty-first year, leaving a widow and five daughters. On the monument which covers his grave in the Armenian cemetery at Madras the following lines are inscribed:—

"Sacred to the memory of JOSEPH MARCUS JOSEPH, M.D., Surgeon-General (Retired), Madras Army, who died at Madras 17th October 1886, aged 60 years and 6 months. This monument is erected in loving remembrance by his sorrowing widow."

At present there are six Armenians in the Indian Medical Service, as below:—

Surg.-Maj. S. T. Avetoom ...	Medical Officer, 27th Bombay Light Infantry, Loralai.
Surg.-Lieut.-Col. J. M. Zorab, M. B.	Civil Surgeon and Superintendent, Orissa Medical School, Cuttack.
Dr. S. J. Manook, M R C.S ...	Sub-Assistant Commissioner, Civil Surgeon and Superintendent of Jail, Chyebassa, Singbhoom.
Surg.-Capt. C. J. Sarkies, M.B.	8th Bombay Infantry, Ahmednagar.
Surg.-Maj. S. C. Sarkies ...	District Surgeon and Superintendent of Jail, Cannanore.
Surgeon-Captain J. G. Jordan	Civil Surgeon and Superintendent of Jail, Backergunj.

* Where his father was an Armenian merchant. His elder brother also carried on, about the middle of the present century, a chemist's business there.

There are but few Armenians as private medical practitioners in India.

The Indian Public Works Department has been another happy hunting-ground for Armenians. Some of them, as Civil Engineers, have rendered valuable services to Government. A notable instance is Mr. J. D. Melik-Beglar, late Executive Engineer and Archæological Surveyor in the Bengal Public Works Department, who has retired at Chogdah on pension. His knowledge of Indian Archæology did not escape the attention of the Bengal Government, and he was placed on special duty, many years ago, to superintend the archæological excavations at the far-famed Buddhist temple at Buddha-Gya. As everyone knows, the temple was reclaimed from oblivion. He had the happiness of enjoying the friendship and tuition of that eminent archæologist, the late talented General Sir Alexander Cunningham, Director-General, Archæological Survey of India. Mr. K. H. Stephen, Under-Secretary, Irrigation Department, Public Works, Bengal, is also an Armenian.

Last, but by no means least, there are two Armenians in the Indian Civil Service, *viz.*:—P. G. Melitus, C.I.E., Deputy Secretary, Government of India, Home Department, and G. Balthazar, Assistant Commissioner, Cachar.

In the good old days, the enterprising Armenians, whose love for commerce is proverbial, were solely engaged in commercial pursuits in India. Being first in the field, they had the running entirely to themselves. They have, generally speaking, been ousted from their position as eminent merchants; yet have not shared the fate of their brother-traders, the Dutch, the Danes, and the

French. They are now following various avocations in rivalry with Europeans in this country, and their probity has gained for them a world-wide reputation. At Calcutta there are still a few Armenian mercantile houses, the chief being the firm of Messrs. Apcar & Co., already referred to at pp. 126-28; and in the following professions and trades they are represented in Calcutta as doctors, honorary magistrates, barristers, solicitors, pleaders, editors, schoolmasters, brokers, underwriters, average-adjusters, chemists and druggists, jewellers and dealers in precious stones, watchmakers, builders and contractors, dealers in curios, cabinet makers, and harness and shoe-makers,—all necessary in a civilised community.

Of all places in India, Calcutta contains by far the largest number of influential and well-to-do Armenians. Here they have a church, a college, an almshouse, an association, and a club of their own. The Armenians in Calcutta now number about seven hundred souls. At other places in India their numbers are but small. In conclusion, it is a noteworthy fact that the early Armenian settlers in India were very conservative in their social habits, and were everywhere recognised by their national costumes; and their ardent love for their Church and national literature have ever been prominent features in their private character. They devoutly performed the various religious rites and ceremonies enjoined by their Church, and instilled into their offspring its dogmas and doctrines. With a praiseworthy zeal they cultivated their national literature, and stimulated its advancement by founding and endowing educational establishments. They were exclusive in their habits. Though engaging freely with their European *confrères* in trade, they did not mix with them socially, and rarely married outside their own nationality. Thereby they preserved their nationalism for many generations; but Time, which brings about wonders, has worked many changes. The national costume has been discarded, except by their clergy; the Armenian language has been almost neglected; and European customs have been generally adopted by the nineteenth-century Armenians.

The result of these changes has been that several Armenians have intermarried with Europeans and Eurasians, and have forsaken their Church for the creed of their wives. But the Armenian community still remains distinct and also somewhat exclusive. It is not likely that they will share the fate of their countrymen at Amsterdam,* Leghorn,† Venice,‡ and at other

* Amsterdam at one time contained an influential Armenian colony, and it was here in 1666 that the *first* Armenian Bible was printed by the zealous Woskan, a learned Armenian monk of Etchmiatzin and a native of Erivan in Armenia. According to the printer's notice, it was published by the hearty co-operation and at the sole expense of Messrs. Stephen, Theodore, and Petrus, three notable Armenian merchants of Julfa, whom he had met at Leghorn on his way to Amsterdam. The printing commenced on 11th March 1666, and was completed on 13th October 1668, the type used in the printing of that and subsequent works having been prepared by the printer's brother, Avetis, who was then a merchant at Amsterdam. This now exceedingly rare Bible is profusely illustrated with fine wood and steel engravings by Dutch artists.

† The Armenian colonists at Leghorn, who were mostly from Julfa and India, were solely engaged in commerce. An Armenian press was also started at Leghorn in 1643 by an Armenian monk named Johanness, a native of Julfa in Ispahan. The first publication issued from it was the Book of Psalms. Other books were subsequently published at that press.

‡ Venice, the Venetik of the Armenians, has played a very prominent part in the history of Armenian literature. The *first* Armenian publication—the Book of Psalms—saw the light there in 1565. It was printed in octavo size by Abgar, surnamed 'the Scribe,' a learned Armenian from Tocat in Armenia. He was a descendant of the former Armenian kings and visited Rome, accompanied by his son, Soolthanshah. From thence they passed to Venice, at that time one of the greatest commercial marts in Europe. There the opulent Armenian merchants, who were chiefly from old Julfa on the Araxes in Armenia, appreciated and encouraged his labours in the cause of the advancement of the national literature.

commercial centres in Europe, where practically they have been absorbed among the people of those countries.

My pleasant task is finished. The reader will now be able to form his own opinion of what the early Armenians have done in helping the British to inaugurate their rule in India, and what claim Armenians generally have upon English sympathy and help, especially in time of trial and difficulty. The sympathy of Christians in all parts of the world has been aroused by the atrocities committed upon Armenians for the sake of their Christian religion, by Turks and Kurds; and we watch with anxiety what will be the issue of the representations of the Great Powers to the Porte. It is earnestly to be hoped that the much-needed reforms in Turkish Armenia will be carried out, and that the condition of the Armenians in that country will be ameliorated and greatly improved.

My readers, I will now say Adieu!

APPENDICES.

APPENDIX A.

THE CLASSICAL ARMENIAN LANGUAGE.

THE following, which appeared as an editorial in the Calcutta *Statesman* on 17th February 1895, has been republished here at the request of several Armenians in Calcutta :—

"The interest aroused in the affairs of Armenia by the misfortunes which have befallen its inhabitants * is probably, from the nature of the case, destined to be, to a certain extent, transient; but there is one possession of the race which is both of world-wide concern and of enduring importance. We refer to the rich literature hidden away in the Armenian language.† It is a treasure which not even the Turks have thought fit to deprive them of, though a considerable portion of the literary heirlooms of the race has long lain at the mercy of their oppressors. Unquestionably, this forbearance has sprung from ignorance; for it is only in recent years that European *savants* themselves have been attracted to the examination of those unsifted hoards. Even at the present day, when the knowledge of what lies in store is spread abroad, the number of European scholars who have taken the trouble to acquire the Armenian language might be counted on the fingers of two hands. These have been Petermann, Neumann,‡ and one or two others in Germany, § Brosset in France, || and Boroeff in Russia; whilst the only English-

---

* This has particular reference to the dreadful tragedy enacted at Sassoon, Armenia, in the autumn of 1894, which shocked the Christian world. The Rev. F. D. Greene, in his illustrated work, *The Armenian Crisis and the Rule of the Turk*, recently published, discusses their daily oppression under Turkish rule.

† Byron, in referring to the Armenian language, said:—"It is a rich language, and would amply repay any one the trouble of learning it."

‡ See page 12, footnote.

§ The greatest of these is undoubtedly Professor Max Müller, the foremost oriental scholar of the present day. He has gained so complete a mastery over classical Armenian as to be able to converse fluently in it.

|| Many other Frenchmen have studied the Armenian language. For instance, James Villote, Mathurin de la Croze (who styled the Armenian version of the Bible as the Queen of all the Versions), Villefroy, abbot of Blamont, St. Martin, Eugène Bore, and Victor Langlois, the distinguished

man * who can be said to have made a real study of the language is Mr. F. Conybeare, of Oxford.† The last-named gentleman has concerned himself chiefly with the Armenian translations of certain works of Greek authors, the originals of which have not come down to our own times. One or two of these were issued last year by the Clarendon Press. Lord Byron was said in his day to have acquired the Armenian tongue, but the assertion rests merely upon his expressed admiration for certain Armenian poems which he

---

scholar and archæologist, who published at Paris in 1867 his *Collection des Historians anciens et modernes de l'Armenie en Français.*

* This is a mistake; for the following Englishmen are known to have studied the Armenian language in the past and present centuries:—William and George Whiston, who published a Latin translation of the History and Geography of Armenia by Moses of Khorene, the father of Armenian historians, who flourished in the fifth century. I possess a copy of this now rare publication, which was printed in London in 1736 with the original Armenian text. The brothers Whiston had learned the Armenian language from their father, Gulielmus Whiston, who had acquired the language in India while he was engaged as a private tutor to the sons of Gregory Agapheerean, an Armenian merchant of Madras. Lord Byron, Edward Lombe, and John Brand, all eminent Englishmen, studied the language with the Mekhitharist Fathers at Venice, whom they helped to publish grammars and dictionaries for the study of the language by Englishmen. The preface to the English-Armenian Dictionary, published at Venice, in 1821, by Father Paschal Aucher, D.D., contains the following:—

"We had been frequently urged by the Armenian subjects of His Britannic Majesty in the East Indies to furnish them by our philological labours with the means of prosecuting advantageously a study of so much consequence to their immediate interests. But as our College at San Lazzaro has in its literary enterprises always needed the assistance of benefactors, so in this important undertaking it required aid and encouragement from without. Such aid and encouragement it has found in the kindness of some English gentlemen. Among these we are proud to name Lord Byron, the most distinguished of the English poets even in the present splendid age of English poetry, who, after having studied Armenian among us, induced us to publish a short Armenian Grammar of the English tongue for the use of Armenians, and also assisted us in the composition of an English Grammar of the Armenian tongue for the use of his own countrymen. Edward Lombe, Esquire, a young gentleman of distinguished talents and fond of the study of languages, afterwards induced us to print the latter. Finally, John Brand, Esquire, Master of Arts of the University of Cambridge, perceiving that the two Grammars were not sufficient to supply the wants of a student, and hearing that we were desirous of composing Dictionaries for the mutual benefit of the English and Armenian nations, promised us his aid in the prosecution of the undertaking."

† This enthusiast, accompanied by his accomplished wife, made a tour through Armenia in 1888, and also came in 1890 to India in quest of old Armenian manuscripts. He visited the Armenian College and Philanthropic Academy, Calcutta, which at one time had on its shelves more than a thousand valuable Armenian volumes, many of them in manuscript. After looking at the title-pages of one or two Armenian books (one of which was printed at Madras in 1773) he desired to see the MSS., and was visibly disappointed on learning that they had long ago disappeared, no one knew whither.

heard of when in Italy * As a matter of fact, the means of learning the language are hardly accessible to Englishmen; and the only grammar is the crude compilation, now out of print, put forth in 1819 by a Mechitarist monk at Venice.†

"Before indicating what are the main contents of Armenian literature, MS. and otherwise, and where these are to be found, it is worth while relating how general attention was in our own time directed to this subject. The convent of San Lazaro, on one of the outer islets off Venice, has for many centuries been a refuge for Armenian monks who had partially conformed to the Roman sway.‡ Here a vast store of MSS. had gradually collected, unheeded by the inmates. In the early part of the present century, however, the monk who wrote the grammar began ransacking these accumulations, and, as there was a press in the establishment, he managed in the course of years to print a few of his discoveries. Still, as the works thus issued were locked up in the unknown Armenian idiom, no real interest was drawn to them. Not until some forty years later was their value made public; and here is the story. It had long been the desire of Christian scholars to find the text of a work frequently referred to by patristic writers and known as the Diatessaron of Tatian. § It was supposed to have been irrecoverably lost; for, although it was a popular book in the early centuries of Christianity, a Greek bishop in the fifth century, deeming it heretical, had ordered every copy that could

---

* This is a fallacy; for Byron studied the classical Armenian language with the Mekhitharist Fathers while he stayed at Venice (see page 149, footnote); and the following letter, which he wrote from that city to Mr. Murray, on the 4th December 1816, shows that, difficult as the language seemed to him, he had determined to master its difficulties:—

"I wrote to you at some length last week, and have little to add, except that I have begun, and am proceeding in a study of the Armenian language, which I acquire, as well as I can, at the Armenian convent, where I go every day to take lessons of a learned friar, and have gained some singular and not useless information with regard to the literature and customs of that oriental people. They have an establishment here—a church and convent of ninety monks, very learned and accomplished men, some of them. They have also a press, and make great efforts for the enlightening of their nation. I find the language (which is twin, the literal and the vulgar) difficult, but not invincible (at least I hope not). *I shall go on.* I found it necessary to twist my mind round some severer study, and this, as being the hardest I could devise here, will be a file for the serpent."

† The Mekhitharist monk referred to in the *Statesman's* excellent article can be no other than Father Paschal Aucher. According to Brand, in his preface to the Armenian-English Dictionary published at Venice in 1825, Father Paschal Aucher was "acquainted with the English language, and, having taught Armenian to Lord Byron, had by his assistance afterwards published a grammar of that tongue for the use of the English." The assistance of Lord Byron in the compilation of that grammar sufficiently warrants the contrary assertion that it was not a "crude compilation."

‡ See page 148, footnote.

§ For fuller information of Tatian's Gospel, see Appendix B.

be found to be burned. Now the main value of the Diatessaron was this: It comprised a harmony of the Four Gospels, and was proved by overwhelming contemporary evidence to have been in circulation at least before the close of the second century. Its worth, as evidence of the contents of the Gospels, as received in sub-Apostolic times, was, therefore, priceless. In 1876 Canon Lightfoot, in an article in the *Contemporary Review*, expressed the hopeless wish that Tatian's composition might still be in existence He little dreamed that, while he was penning these words, the prize he longed for actually lay in the room in which he was writing. On the top shelf of his book-case were a couple of badly-printed Armenian volumes which he had picked up as a sort of curiosity at a second-hand shop in Italy. In these was the priceless treasure which the whole theological world desired! In the Venetian convent where the old monk worked, had long lain a MS. copy of an Armenian translation of the Diatessaron made prior to the general order for its destruction. That copy had been found and printed by the monk, though even he knew little of its value. It was not until two or three years after Lightfoot wrote his article that, by accident, he learnt the contents of the volumes on his top shelf; but now they have been re-published in German, we believe, and are well known as formidable evidence in New Testament criticism. But this discovery had influence beyond the immediate object found. It brought about a more accurate investigation of the whole subject of Armenian literature; the cataloguing * of all Armenian MSS. in European libraries, and visits of scholars to the principal monasteries in Armenia itself.

"The writings extant in the Armenian language may be divided into two great departments. In the first should be placed the vast series of translations of classical and theological works made in the early centuries of the Christian era. In the second comes the great body of indigenous compositions, chiefly history and poetry, the original produce of native Armenian talent. Undoubtedly the first-mentioned class is more valuable of the two, its principal worth consisting in the number of standard works of the great ancients still to be found in Armenian dress, although the originals have long since perished. We owe this department to the excessive admiration which characterised the earlier days of literary activity in Armenia for anything written in the Greek or Latin tongue. A mania for translation set in during the fifth and sixth centuries A.D., which was perfectly indiscriminating. Everything in those languages then existing, masterpieces and rubbish alike, was ferreted out and diligently rendered into Armenian. As so much was then available which has not sur-

* The lists of the Armenian MSS. at St Petersburg and in the Vatican Library were compiled by the learned Mekhitharist Fathers at Vienna.

vived in any other form, the result has been to preserve for our own day not only what is valuable in the literatures of Greece and Rome, but also much that is merely curious and interesting. The multitude of copies made of the same writings—for every Armenian monastery had its battalion of copyists—has contributed, moreover, to the completeness of these series of survivals. We have here not only all the works of Aristotle, Plato, Cicero, Isocrates, and even of Juvenal, Terence, and Aristophanes; but also the entire phalanx of Greek theological writers of the Christian age.* Secular and sacred literature are fully and equally represented. So far as these versions have been examined, they have yielded results in a double way—both in the critical emendation of existing texts and in the recovery of lost books and missing portions. However, as we have already said, the whole field has as yet been comparatively little explored; mines of archæological and literary wealth remain still absolutely unworked. Probably much of value continues hidden away and undiscovered. As to the second department of Armenian writings, that which is the production of original authorship, investigation here has been equally limited. Exhaustive examination of none of them, save the few which have been rendered into German, has been ever attempted. Numerous narratives of the Mongol conquests in the Middle Ages were written in Armenian, but so far European historians have been unable to utilise them. Regarding the whereabouts of these literary treasures, little can be set down in the present cursory account. The principal emporium in Armenia itself is the library of the great monastery at Echmiadzin.† Archbishop Sarghis, also, is said to have an important collection at Sanahin, his private property. Moreover, most of the numerous convents in the country possess libraries, large or small. There are many depositories of Armenian MSS. in Europe. Such are the libraries at Venice, Lemberg, Vienna,‡

---

* See Appendix B.

† A complete list of the Armenian MSS. in the library at Etchmiatzin (which, according to Mr. Conybeare, contains 4 000 MSS) is now being compiled for publication by the Rev. Dr. Mesrovb Ter Mosesean, who has also prepared the list of the Armenian MSS. in the National Library (Bibliothèque Nationale) at Paris.

‡ The learned Mekhitharist Fathers at Vienna have just published a very valuable list (1,000 pages) of about 500 Armenian MSS., which they possess in the archives of their own library, with a preface in German. It is dedicated to their worthy abbot, His Grace the Very Rev. Father Arsen Aidnean, an eminent scholar and the greatest Armenian grammarian of the present day, on the occasion of his episcopal and literary jubilee on 3rd November 1895. As an enthusiastic admirer of the classical language of ancient Armenia, the writer embraces this opportunity of congratulating the venerable abbot and wishing him many years of further usefulness.

and Moscow; and the private collections of Mr. Emin* at Moscow and M. Khoodobasheff at St. Petersburg. Our British Museum in London is possessed of fifty-four works, all, however, of little value; and in Madras there is another Armenian collection.

"The study of the Armenian language and literature, it will thus be seen, is well worthy of serious attention. Furthermore, the storehouses of its treasures lie comparatively near at hand. When even women, in their pursuit of learning, brave the perils of the Sinaitic desert, the wonder is that the field in this case should remain vacant. For Armenians themselves, who, as in India, know both English and their own idiom,† there is here a magnificent opening. We hear of a revival of interest in their own language among the Armenians of Calcutta. Indeed, one young lady is now busy rescuing from oblivion the ancient melodies and chants used in the Armenian Church and handed down hitherto only orally. She is, we believe, not merely reducing them to modern musical notation, but, finding no music-printers in Calcutta, has imported her own type and is setting it up herself. We are informed, too, that in the Free School a class for special instruction in Armenian has been for some time in progress; certain Armenian ladies bearing the necessary expense. Is it too much to hope that the same patriotic spirit which has prompted these efforts may find further expression in a greater undertaking, and that the patient endeavours of the old Armenian copyists to preserve the treasures of antiquity from destruction may be crowned by those of the modern Armenian scholar to restore them to the world?"

---

* Mr. Emin died a few years ago at Moscow, where for many years he had been a professor at the Lazareff College, founded in 1815 by the opulent Lazars—Armenian merchants of Julfa, who had settled at Moscow in the eighteenth century. Mr. Emin was an eminent scholar and the author of several learned works on the history and literature of Armenia. A native of Julfa, he had received his primary education at the feet of the late Johanness Avdall at the Armenian Philanthropic Academy, Calcutta. Leaving this city in 1825, he went to Moscow, there to complete his studies at the Lazareff College, where he laboured all the days of his life. He was a bachelor, and bequeathed his fortune for the furthering of his national literature.

† The Armenians in India have, for the past fifty years, neglected the study of classical Armenian; and even colloquial or modern Armenian is becoming more and more neglected, the present generation of Armenians in India, with a few exceptions, being unable freely to converse in it.

APPENDIX B.

A NEGLECTED CLASSICAL LANGUAGE.

THE Rev. Graham Sandberg, B.A., LL.B., at present Military Chaplain at Subathu, writes in the *Calcutta Review* for July 1891:—

"As is now the method of attack adopted in one department of Old Testament analysis, so was there, then, a loud malignant whisper which talked of a common ancestral 'document' from which the Gospel writers had drawn and misdrawn their 'facts.' It was a 'Compendium of the Life of Jesus Christ,' by one Tatian, to which Eusebius had referred, and which was in extensive circulation in the second century in the Syrian Church, which many of the critics seized upon as the probable quarry from which the Evangelists had picked out a harmonious substratum on which to build the bulwarks of Christianity. Bishop Lightfoot, however, had a subtler theory than that. 'No,' said he, 'this work of Tatian shall, indeed, form a foundation for the Gospels, but only as fixing a chronological barrier, marking a date, before which they must have been composed.' Thence he went on to demonstrate the probability that Tatian's work was compounded out of the Gospels, not the Gospels out of Tatian. Now, if this theory could have been proved to be fact by the worthy Bishop, it would have established an irrefragable position—namely, that the Evangelist's narratives, from which Tatian copied, must have been in existence previous to the year 160 A.D., the acknowledged latest date for Tatian's Compendium. The Bishop guessed this work to be merely a harmony of the Four Gospels; but he could not prove it so, and thus establish the prior appearance of the Gospels, because the work itself had been lost for centuries, so that its exact contents were thus unknown. And here comes in the romance of the story. 'Ah! if Tatian's work could only be recovered from the bygone ages to confirm the truth!' must have often been the learned writer's craving. But that was almost impossible. Even Eusebius, in the fifth century, could only describe the book from hearsay. When Theodopetus, Bishop of Cyrrhus, visited in the year 280 the Syrian Church in Edessa, he had ordered all copies of 'Tatian's Gospel' to be destroyed as heretical. Notwithstanding, then, the hopelessness of recovering the lost treasure in the nineteenth century, will the real situation be credited? The case was actually this: while Dr. Lightfoot was penning his famous articles, the longed-for work was in reality stowed away on the top shelf of his bookcase!

"Prior to the destruction of Tatian's Gospel, one Ephraem, the Syrian, had embodied, paragraph by paragraph, the entire work in a Commentary which he had composed upon it. He wrote in Syriac, and his compilation had also long ago disappeared. However, in the days when it was popular, Ephraem's work had been translated into the Armenian language. The Armenian version had not been lost; but Armenian was—and is—a language unknown to our theologians. An Armenian monk of the convent established by Mekhithar at Venice, by name Paschal Aucher, had even published Ephraem's Commentary in 1832; little dreaming of its value. Bishop Lightfoot, many years previously, in a bibliophilist humour, had purchased a second-hand copy in Venice, meaning some day to study Armenian. Yet it was not by the Bishop that these circumstances were brought to light. In 1877, a German lighted upon Aucher's publication at Venice; and it was only when this discovery was revealed to the world of letters that Dr. Lightfoot found on his book-shelf his own copy. It remained for the learned scholar Theodor Zahn to pick out Tatian's Gospel—the Diatessaron, as it is styled—piece by piece from Ephraem's Commentary, and, putting the paragraphs together, to make public the ancient work in its entirety once again. Then, indeed, was Lightfoot's conjecture proved to be correct. Tatian had merely aimed at presenting a full and consecutive narrative of Christ's Life, by linking together into one whole all the important statements and facts recited by the four Evangelists. Their very words were culled bodily by this second century harmonist, and the antiquity of the Gospels, as Lightfoot had anticipated, was indisputably settled by these voluminous quotations.

"To the Armenians and their language is this important result primarily due. Moreover, we have introduced the long, but interesting, narrative only with the intention of leading up to the subject of this review, which is designed to set forth the importance of this neglected tongue to English students.

"Armenian is a language which deserves to be seriously studied by both the theological and the classical scholar. Hidden away in this idiom,—and, again, hidden away in the libraries of obscure Armenian monasteries—exist treasures of ancient literature, indigenous as well as imported, which would adequately repay the trouble and patience of mastering a new language of certainly exceptional difficulty.

. . . .

"In the fourth century of the Christian era the Armenian idiom was elevated to the dignity of a written language, Greek having been previously the literary medium of Armenian scholars. When the language had thus gained a character of its own, a veritable bibliomania almost immediately set in. Throughout the fifth and following centuries, so amazing was the national voracity for books of all kinds, that a perfect army of scribes in every convent were put to attack the literatures of all countries. In that way, the whole body of Greek and Syriac works, sacred and profane, then current, was presently transferred into the Armenian tongue. So omnivorous were the translators, that writings, important and insignificant, were indiscriminately seized upon and duly assimilated, one and all, to the vernacular idiom. As a result, many of the minor compositions of ancient authors, which have been long ago lost in their original forms, are now found existing in these Armenian translations in old monastic libraries. In an age, like our own, which is so ingenious in erecting magnificent fabrics out of forgotten rubbish heaps, such materials will be considered more important than any discovery of *opera majora*. At least it is a consolation to surmise that certain of the books which the destruction of the famous Alexandrian Library was supposed to have removed for ever from the world, may yet be found mouldering in damp chambers on the crags around Ararat.

"Some of the more prominent of the translations made from the Greek in the fifth century may now be enumerated. Armenian editions of at least five of the works of Aristotle are known to survive, namely, the Categories, the Analytikon, Περι Κοσμον, Περι Αρητην and Περί Ερμηνειας. It is the Armenian version of these works which Mr. Conybeare has collated and published. Then we have the complete productions of the poet Kallimachos, the writings of Diodoros Sikulos, Olympiodoros, and four volumes of Aeschylos. A voluminous life of Alexander the Great, by an anonymous Greek author, is among the MSS. at Venice. All the ordinary Greek classics are likewise to be met with.

"The editions of the Fathers and the Ecclesiastical Historians are the most notable treasures. Amongst those specially worth examination and collation are the five series of the works of St. Athanasius. The Armenian copies represent translations made within 100 years from the date of that great author's death, recording, therefore, his *ipsisima verba* before the corruptions and perversions of later editions were put forth. At Venice exist MSS. of 23 separate works of Athanasius, including his 'Life of St. Anthony, the Abbot, and other Holy Anchorites,' and the disputed tract on the Incarnation; also the Missal and Breviary said to have been the compilations of the saint. Philo's works have a peculiar interest; and the Armenians can boast here certain survivals not known to exist in any other form. I can only mention the writings of this author existing in the Mekhitar College at Venice; but others are reported from the Archiepiscopal Library at Erivan. The Venice series of Philo comprises :—

(1) Three Dialogues : one on the Souls of Beasts, and two on the Providence of God.

(2) Researches on the Books of Genesis and Exodus.
(3) Discourses on Samson and Jonah.
(4) On the three Angels which appeared to Abraham.

"Of ancient books which have acquired a mysterious reputation, chiefly because they were numbered amongst the 'lost,' none seem to be so often referred to as the 'Chronicle' of Eusebius of Cæsarea. Until comparatively recent times, this work was only known through Jerome's account of it, and was said to consist of an elaborate chronology, preceded by an epitome of universal history. Scaliger endeavoured to compile a supposititious text of the chronicle, using the various extracts from it, as given by contemporary authors. However, in 1788, an Armenian version of the original was found in St. James's Monastery at Jerusalem; whilst, later, an Armenian translation of a Syriac version came to light from Etchmiadzin. Careful collations of these MSS. were not made until eighty years afterwards, by Petermann; and now, with the help of Jerome's text, we may at last be said to have had this not very important mystery solved and to have been put in possession of Eusebius's work exactly as it was left by its author. Naturally there are innumerable writings by St. Chrysostom to be met with in Armenian dress. It would require the scrutiny of an expert to pick out any of those which do not survive in their original Greek, if any such there be. Chrysostom has, I fancy, been too universally popular in the Eastern Churches for even one of his minor compositions to have been permitted to lie in oblivion and so become lost. Nevertheless, it may be of interest to name some of the titles occurring in Somal's Italian list:—

(1) Commentary on St. Matthew.
(2) Thirty-three Homilies on St. John's Gospel.
(3) Homilies on St. Paul's Epistles.
(4) On the Annunciation.
(5) On the Holy Cross.
(6) Homilies on St. Thomas's Unbelief and concerning the Sunday known as *Dominica in Albis*.
(7) On St. Milesius, Bishop of Antioch.
(8) On the Baptism of Jesus Christ.
(9) On Penitence and the Prophet Jonah.
(10) On the Passover of the Hebrews.
(11) On the Good Samaritan.

"Turning to the Epistles of Ignatius, Bishop of Antioch, which, as documents composed only eighty years after the Crucifixion, are of the utmost importance in the determination of many nice points of primitive Christian doctrines, and of early Church government, the famous controversy as to the original shape of these letters will at once recur to the student's mind. Cureton's theory that the Ignatian Epistles were originally only three in number (which was so eagerly caught at and enlarged upon, *contr.*

Christianos, by Bunsen and Renan) has been at length most conclusively refuted. Zahn, Lightfoot, and Dr. Travers Smith of Dublin, have caused the majority of critical scholars to accept, as the genuine productions of the venerable martyr, the seven somewhat shortened letters which Vossius first disinterred from the Medicean MS. Few, however, are aware of the important confirmation of these conclusions to be gathered from Armenian sources. The Armenian version contains the seven Epistles, in shortened form, and entirely free from the Arian interpolations which first cast discredit on the expanded editions. As the Armenians derived their series from the Syriac early in the fifth century, this version reaches back almost to the times of Eusebius, with whose extracts and comments it exactly harmonizes. In addition to the seven accepted Epistles, we find, in the Armenian series, the six other letters usually held to be spurious. Nevertheless, as these six non-Ignatian Epistles were evidently translated in one batch with the genuine letters, which had not then (as this version plainly proves) been manipulated by the Arian interpolator, we at least ascertain that the six were not, as was once supposed, further compositions of the heretical interpolator, but that they are—though not of Ignatian authorship—yet *of very early origin*. These last are thus intituled in the Armenian collection :—(1) To those of Antioch ; (2) From Mary, the Proselyte of Kasdapagha, to Ignatius ; (3) Reply of Ignatius ; (4) To those of Tarsus ; (5) To the Deacon Heron of Antioch ; (6) To the Phillippians.

"Our orthodox Churches, doubtless, have pardonable cause for triumph in the establishment of the authenticity of this famous septet of second-century letters, as opposed to Cureton's excerpts. Many are the important positions and doctrines which thereby gain the strength of the stainless testimony of a 'Pupil of St. John' as to their being current in the most primitive ages of Christianity. Some of those conclusions deserve special mention here. The Ignatian Epistles, when the unadulterated versions of Armenia and Syria are consulted, at least establish :—

(1) That there existed in the Church of the first quarter of the second century the three Orders—of Bishop, Priest, and Deacon.

(2) That the New Testament was, for Ignatius and also for the Church of his time, already a written collection like the Old.

(3) That the Old Testament had the solemn imprimatur of re-adoption by the Churches, as the direct Revelation of God. so early as 110 A.D. at least.

(4) That the Holy Communion occupied then a commanding position : the word *Eucharist* being reserved to express only a specified section of the office.

(5) That the Christians had already cast aside the Jewish Sabbath, and observed, as the Lord's Day, the first day of the week.

(6) The writers of that day were familiar with the phrase 'the Catholic Church.'

"Moreover, in quitting this most interesting of subjects, and one very properly interminable to the Christian apologist, it is worth pointing out, as one of the more important pieces of internal testimony to their antiquity, that the word 'Trinity' is not once mentioned in these writings, just as it is absent from the canonical works of the New Testament. Nevertheless, as in the latter, the particulars of the doctrine are as fully and palpably implied.

"Extraordinary, indeed, is the mass of patristic literature thus lying *perdu* in this unknown tongue. Much of it, doubtless, is unworthy of translation; but, on the other hand, much would prove of the highest value for critical and collative purposes, if only it were rendered available to the professional analyst. For example, of the works of Ephraem, the Syrian, twenty-nine volumes are known to exist in Armenian MSS., in addition to the valuable Commentary on Tatian's harmony. The writings of Eusebius Emesenus, of which nothing but a few fragments have been hitherto seen by European scholars, are to be found in their entirety in the Ararat monasteries. I must also mention having noticed the occurrence of no fewer than 34 volumes of St. Gregory Nazianzen, 17 treatises by St. Basil, and the rare works of Timothy, Patriarch of Alexandria, in the Armenian lists. However, enough of this. My object is not to catalogue exhaustively, but only to indicate generally, and to lead the way to further investigations by future possible students.

. . . .

"But where are these relics of past industry and learning to be met with? All the leading libraries of Europe have been endowed with moderate collections of books and MSS. in the language; and the majority of such possessions have been subjected to some sort of examination by competent scholars. In the British Museum, there seem to be about 52 Armenian MSS., in addition of course to a large series of printed works issued in recent years from modern Armenian presses in Russia and Turkey. The MSS. are mostly copies of the four Gospels written in several characters and illuminated, together with a few ancient specimens of missals and hymn books. Two or three of the Gospel MSS. are of value, as they were penned in the tenth and eleventh centuries, and are written on a curious thick cotton paper. Several theological works are included in the British Museum collection; likewise a very ancient copy of a Commentary on the Psalms, dating from the twelfth century, and a Life of St. John the Evangelist, in a copy marked with an Armenian date corresponding to the year 1307 of our era. A thirteenth century copy of the Apocalypse and Epistles includes an apochryphal epistle from the Corinthians to St. Paul, with the Apostle's letter in reply. At Oxford the Archives of the Bodleian Library hold a goodly number of MSS., rather more varied in character than those in London. They have been of late submitted to the critical scrutiny of Dr. S. Baronian* of Manchester, who has already in the Press a full descriptive catalogue. Other European collections of Armenian treasures are to be found in the Bibliotheque Nationale at Paris, in the San Lazaro Convent of Venice, where are 383 MSS., in the Armenian Monastery at Vienna, in the Vatican Library (13 MSS) at Lemberg Monastery in Galicia, and in the Lazarev Institute at Moscow. Besides these, several private collections are in existence, among which special mention may be made of that of M. Emin at Moscow, that of Gospodin Khoodobashey at St. Petersburg, and that of an Armenian gentleman residing at Cairo, referred to by Mr. Conybeare.

"But the principal hunting-ground for the antiquarian and the original investigator must be the country itself, although it is just possible that a few treasures lie hidden in our Indian libraries. All the larger, and some of the minor, monasteries in Armenia Proper can boast of book hoards, the contents of which deserve inspection. Many of these storehouses of bygone learning have never been visited by travellers or even by Armenians of any education. The central establishment of this kind, without doubt, is the Patriarchal Monastery of Etchmiadzin. There resides the head of the whole Armenian Orthodox Church, now, indeed, a venerable patriarch in the truest sense, being upwards of 90 years of age.† Mr. Conybeare, who visited the monastery in 1888, remarks: 'Vagharshapad, the Armenian village which has grown up round the monastery, is a poor place, consisting of mud-built houses. The chief building, after the monastery, is the college, a long copper-roofed stone edifice, in which are educated about 200 Armenian youths, who come from both Turkey and Russia. There is a fine library, well stocked with books of re-

* The Rev Dr. Sookeas Baronian is in spiritual charge of the flourishing Armenian colony at Manchester, who are solely engaged in commerce.

† This refers to the late Catholicos. His Holiness Makar, who died at Etchmiatzin in 1891. The present head of the orthodox Armenian Church is His Holiness Mgrtich I., who was consecrated Catholicos of all Armenia on 8th October 1893 at Etchmiatzin. By his unaffected devotion and true patriotism, he has won the enthusiastic admiration of the entire Armenian nation, and is known by the endearing name of *Hairik'* (*i.e.*, Little Father). This venerable ecclesiastic is now in his seventy-fifth year, and may God extend the golden thread of his useful life for the glory of His Church and the benefit of the Armenian nation.

ference.' The writer adds, 'that the monastic library contains some 4,000 manuscripts—a statement which is hardly to be reconciled with the estimate of 481 MSS. as given by M. Brosset. At Erivan, with its enchanting views of Mount Ararat (18,800 feet above sea-level), is a private library, containing many unique works, the property of Mons. Voskan Wohannesiantz. At Sanahin is the fine collection of over 100 MSS., known as the library of Archbishop Sarghis. We mention these instances as the chief among many. At Tiflis, where there is a University, we find, of course, an extensive Armenian library, the contents of which are, however, mostly modern productions.'

"So far, this article has treated of the literary treasures known to exist, or likely to be discovered, set forth in the idiom and characters proper to the land of Ararat. But of this neglected language itself we have as yet said nothing, though it is placed as the title of our article. Nevertheless, we hope we have taken decidedly the best course to whet the appetite of the possible student, by exposing to view the inside of the citadel, before the difficulties of ascent thereto are put in sight. We have shown in this way that the language is worth learning; that the literature to which it would yield access is one not without possible prizes, and is deserving to be ransacked and sifted by the antiquarian, the classical scholar and the theological student."

THE END.